All About Politics

ALL ABOUT POLITICS

Questions and Answers
on the U.S. Political Process

PAUL A. THEIS

WILLIAM P. STEPONKUS

R. R. BOWKER COMPANY
New York & London, 1972
A Xerox Education Company

Published by R. R. Bowker Co. (a Xerox Education Company)
1180 Avenue of the Americas, New York, N.Y. 10036
Copyright © 1972 by Xerox Corporation
Printed and bound in the United States of America.

Library of Congress Cataloging in Publication Data

Theis, Paul A.   1923–
    All about politics.

    1. Politics, Practical.   2. United States—
Politics and government.   I. Steponkus, William P.,
1935–   joint author.   II. Title.
JK1726.T48   320   72–8470
ISBN 0–8352–0528–2

Contents

Foreword by Robert Dole   vii

Foreword by Jean Westwood   ix

Preface   xi

PART 1   *Politics: Everybody's Business*   1

     Chapter 1   *What's it all about?*   3

     Chapter 2   *Are political parties necessary?*   26

     Chapter 3   *Why get involved?*   51

PART 2   *Politics: Campaigning for Office*   69

     Chapter 4   *What's the voter like?*   71

     Chapter 5   *What makes a successful campaign?*   89

     Chapter 6   *What laws govern politics?*   112

PART 3   *Politics: Checks and Balances*   133

     Chapter 7   *What makes Congress work?*   135

     Chapter 8   *What about the presidency?*   159

     Chapter 9   *What's ahead?*   186

Selected bibliography   215

Index   219

Foreword

All About Politics is just what its title suggests.

Even to someone in the business of politics for what seems to be too long, I found it not only interesting but informative. I was reminded, too, that the great breadth of the subject probably will consign politics to the status of an art forever rather than a science, the plethora of computers and technical innovations notwithstanding.

The writers have done a well-researched job which avoids the tediousness too frequently found in such writings. In fact, I was struck by the clarity which marked it from start to finish. I suspect that the little things that comprise this business—and there are literally thousands of them—are rather dull to the general reader. Who really cares to know what the specific requirements are of a campaign? And what could be more likely to cause a severe case of ennui than a detailed discussion of the specifics of federal campaign finance legislation? Paul Theis and Bill Steponkus, both with the experience of having been working journalists and political hands, succeed in straining out the chaff in producing this engaging compendium.

Politics is the steaming, snorting, hard-driving engine of government. This book provides a broad but uncluttered look around the cab of that sophisticated madhouse. What is revealed is much of the unglimpsed truth about the basic aspects of the system which have made our democracy the grand and unique example of workable self-government.

I think this book will help to generate both interest in and understanding of politics, particularly for those who *wished* they knew more about it but have been put off by the seeming formidability of the task.

All About Politics removes much of this apprehension and could serve to motivate people to study the political system even further. And that would be good for the system *and* the country.

Senator Robert Dole, *Chairman*
Republican National Committee

Foreword

Few subjects have been as exhaustively covered in print as politics. Aside from contemporary analyses, the American way of electing governments by now would surely be an unfruitful field to plow.

The authors of this book, however, have put that reflection to rest in a spirited, provocative and non-partisan format which is highly informative and entertaining. Whether the reader be a political novice or a professional, there is much hard information in this book about the American political process, compiled in such a way that neither party comes out looking better or worse than the other—no small achievement, incidentally.

Those of us who engage in this invigorating and sometimes frustrating art often overlook the fact that many of our fellow citizens view politics as an unfathomable maze. This view is more often than not based on either lack of information or misunderstanding. As a result, the system we work within is often looked upon, at best, as a creature of our own convenience into which intruders are not welcome and, at worst, with suspicion and distrust.

This book helps to dispel the notion of exclusivity, suggesting reasons why citizens *should* become involved and ways to do it. We in the Democratic Party have already made efforts to broaden this involvement—and we, therefore, welcome these suggestions as well as the convincing arguments in favor of continuation of the two parties and their importance to the system.

This book also emphasizes this vital point: Politics is no better or no worse than the people who become involved in it. It suggests that we get the kind of government we deserve. And vice versa. In short, it's up to us.

MRS. JEAN WESTWOOD, *Chairman*
Democratic National Committee

Preface

Why should I get involved in politics? What's in it for me? Are political parties really necessary? Which is most important in a campaign—the candidate or the issues? Will the Congressional seniority system be replaced? If so, with what? What changes are in store for the American political system? Is a national primary to select presidential candidates a good idea? Should the Electoral College be abolished?

These and several hundred other queries like them provided the genesis of this book. After research confirmed our suspicion that no single up-to-date compilation of the most frequently asked questions about politics existed, the idea for such a book began to take on shape and form.

We started to compile a list. Members of Congress, political professionals and newcomers, friends and associates, all were asked to help identify the areas of political activity they felt were either unknown or little understood. Interestingly, one of the most frequently asked questions of members of the U.S. House of Representatives is: "When are you up for re-election?" This pointed up one basic, but common, area of misunderstanding of the system—for the *entire* House of Representatives is on the ballot every two years.

Before long, the list of questions exceeded 400. The tendency to compose essay-answers was particularly hard to resist when discussing the subtleties of politics or the complexities of compaign legislation or the uncertainties of what the future holds. But the decision was made to adhere to a tightly written question-and-answer format, conversational in style. High on the list of reasons was that of readability; another was the increasing popularity of this approach to knowledge by the press and publishers.

All About Politics is intended to help the reader better understand the American political system. In this sense, it is both a primer and a textbook, a compendium and an analysis, an inquiry and a dialogue. We have tried to keep it concise yet lively—but above all candid and informative.

Since politics is an art rather than a science, there are no right or wrong answers to some of the questions posed—but simply the best judgment of the authors or others we quote or credit. Some readers may, therefore, disagree with answers given or conclusions drawn—and perhaps they well should. But beyond that, we hope, wistfully perhaps, that motivation to become involved in the political process might come to some who otherwise may not have considered the idea.

The way in which America's political leaders are chosen is at times complicated and cumbersome, tempestuous and time-consuming. But, basically, it works. And since it is people-oriented, we believe, from our experience in politics, that the nation will benefit markedly if more people become active participants rather than remaining passive observers. In that way, the system will better represent the electorate and reflect its views. And that's what politics in this country is really all about.

PAUL A. THEIS
Public Relations Director
Republican Congressional Committee

WILLIAM P. STEPONKUS
Executive Assistant to
Congressman Charles W. Whalen, Jr.

PART 1

Politics: Everybody's Business

CHAPTER 1

What's it all about?

How would you assess the state of American politics today?

The U.S. political system is suffering from a bad case of neglect, aggravated by events of the past decade. In brief, it is alive but not entirely well.

What's needed is basic—a massive infusion of citizen participation. Even in a presidential election year, just over 60 percent of Americans eligible to vote actually do so, compared with turnouts of up to 95 percent in Australia, 92 percent in Italy, 90 percent in Austria, and 85 percent in Finland.

But voting participation isn't the only answer. The sad fact is that less than one American in thirty has anything whatever to do with politics—with candidate selection, campaign involvement, issue research, fundraising, or the thousand other activities which go into electing the best men and women to government.

The problem has been compounded over the past decade or so by United States involvement in a seemingly interminable war abroad and the concomitant intensification of other difficulties at home. To the concerned, of which there are far too few, as well as to the indifferent, of which there are far too many, the system was to blame; it just wasn't working.

The effect of all this on the American political system deeply disturbed students of government and leaders in both major parties. Some detected a flickering in the flame of democracy, a disinclination to confront the uncomfortable.

Actually, what is happening today isn't new. In 1940, six months before the United States entered World War II, columnist Walter Lippmann told his Harvard class reunion that Americans had taken the "good things" for granted too long, and "now you must earn them again."

He added, "For every right that you cherish, you have a duty which you must fulfill. For every hope that you entertain, you have a task you must perform. For every good that you wish to preserve, you will have to sacrifice your comfort and ease. There is nothing for nothing any longer."

Thirty-two years later, *Washington Post* political correspondent David S. Broder, in his book *The Party's Over*, put it this way:

> The cost of being an American citizen is going up. If this nation is to survive and meet its responsibilities, many of us will have to sacrifice some of our personal luxuries to help pay for the society's neglected needs. What is more, we will have to give up the idea that we can escape from the consequences of our civic irresponsibility by purchasing private passage for our families to the segregated suburbs, to the private schools and to the protected professions. It is going to cost us time and energy and thought, diverted from private concerns, to make government workable and politics responsible again in America. Our parties, our government will be no more representative than we make them, by our own commitment and participation.

What's wrong with American politics? Nothing fatal, in our view, that citizen involvement can't cure. The system has its share of parasites, pariahs, opportunists, demagogues, incompetents, and crooks, all a big part of the problem. It also has more than its share of good men and women of principle and conviction who aver that America is governable and improvable. And the fact is that government can be changed simply by electing officials dedicated to change, whether they be members of the Berkeley City Council or the president of the United States.

What motivates people to get into politics? Is it power, prestige, public service, money—what?

It's usually a combination of the first three, and the order in which these rank depends upon the individual. Although politicians frequently will say they were motivated to get into politics by a desire to serve the public, the fact is that most ended up there because politics offered them a unique opportunity for fulfillment—a challenge to their ambitions, the stimulation that flows from power or the proximity to power, and the reward that comes from public recognition of their achievements. The personal satisfaction which results from being able to perform a real service to their country or constituents often comes later and is one reason many stay in politics.

Unlike certain professions or business activities, very few people go into politics to get rich, and those who do usually fail or end up in jail. This doesn't suggest that self-interest isn't often a motive for political activity any more than self-advantage isn't a motive for entering law, medicine, or the TV repair business. But it does suggest that the person who goes into politics solely for what he can get out of it monetarily will find there's ample room for him—at the bottom! The economics of political life, in short, are about the same as for life in general; you get out of it roughly what you put in.

Where do the terms "politics" and "politician" come from?

The term "politics," relating to the art and science of government, is derived from the Greek word *polis*, which means city. Originally, a politician was someone who helped manage the affairs of a city.

Today, politics carries a much broader connotation, touching in some form or another every part of human life. It is, in fact, everybody's business. To propose eliminating politics from government is to overlook the fact that politics *is* government—government in action.

The word politician has also been broadened to include anyone who is involved in a career in government, usually in an elected or appointed capacity and ordinarily outside of civil service, or anyone who is engaged in party politics as a professional. The shortened version of politician, "pol," is little employed these days and indicates a superficial knowledge of politics on the part of the user. In fact, "pol" is sometimes resented by professionals who accept the term politician but dislike its abbreviated slang version.

What qualities are needed to be a good politician?

First and foremost is the will to succeed. That's one common trait shared by the men and women who have been successful in politics. The second is a genuine concern for people and their problems and a real interest in helping them find solutions.

Aside from that, the fledgling politician should have experience as an administrator or at least an adaptability for administration. He should be an adequate public speaker and enjoy the limelight which political life thrusts upon its practitioners. He should have the tact of a diplomat and the warmth and understanding of a human relations counselor. In addition, and perhaps most important, he should have a thick skin and the ability to roll with the punches which will surely be thrown at him. As President Harry Truman once sagely observed, "If you can't stand the heat, get out of the kitchen."

What's your definition of an "ideal" politician?

Rather than ours, here's a little-known definition from one leading practitioner of politics, President Nixon. He puts it this way:

> A politician knows that more important than the bill that is proposed is the law that is passed.
> A politician knows that his friends are not always his allies, and that his adversaries are not his enemies.
> A politician knows how to make the process of democracy work and loves the intricate workings of the democratic system.
> A politician knows not only how to count votes, but to make his vote count.
> A politician knows that his words are his weapons, but that his word is his bond.
> A politician knows that only if he leaves room for discussion and room for concession can he gain room for maneuver.
> A politician knows that the best way to be a winner is to make the other side feel it does not have to be a loser.
> And a politician . . . knows both the name of the game and the rules of the game, and he seeks his ends through the time-honored democratic means.

Okay, that may be the ideal, but is it realistic? In other words, I've always heard that politics is a dirty business. True or not?

An oversimplified answer is yes and no.

Since there is no way to guarantee the nobility of men and women who aspire to and reach positions of responsibility in any walk of life, there is likewise no way to assure the morality of citizens who become active in political life. They will always be plagued by the same temptations that brought down Adam and Eve. A few will allow their selfishness and greed to overcome the moral responsibility to the offices they hold. But this number is far less than most Americans realize. And the vigilance of the press doubtless acts as a constraint on temptations which may arise.

Actually, the number of politicians convicted of wrongdoing is smaller proportionately than the number of persons convicted of crimes in business, the professions, and other areas of life. The chief difference is that the conviction of a politician or public official makes headline news while that of a private citizen doesn't. In short, one highly publicized case of wrongdoing by a politician tends to spread the belief that all politicians are crooked.

Is politics a dirty business? Dr. Lee C. McDonald, writing in *Student's Guide to Practical Politics*, replies this way:

> If you mean by "dirty" that politicians are mostly a bunch of crooks for whom graft is a profitable sideline or that crucial elections are often won by stuffing the ballot box, then the answer is no. As a group, politicians are probably as honest in their dealings with other people as bottle-cap manufacturers, deep-sea divers, or college professors. Besides bribery is not in good taste these days. Among political leaders and workers you will find realists and idealists, egotists and altruists, heathens and Christians, bright boys and knuckleheads. If anything, they will be a little more human than usual.

How about this one: "In politics, it isn't what you know, but who you know." Is this true?

This concept is a hangover from the 1800s when President Andrew Jackson introduced the spoils system into government appointments. In those days, federal jobs were used as a payoff to loyal party workers, and it was important to know the right people in political life to obtain one of the jobs. In fact, the phrase "to the victor belong the spoils" was first used in 1832 by Sen. William Marcy of New York in defending President Jackson's appointment of Martin Van Buren as ambassador to Great Britain.

Other presidents continued the practice. For instance, of the approximately 50,000 postmasters across the country in 1889, President Benjamin Harrison changed three out of five during his first year in office, and President Grover Cleveland appointed Democrats to nearly 50,000 of the 57,000-plus civilian government jobs during his first two years in office.

Because of its excesses, the spoils system soon became the target of reformers. The result was the establishment of a merit-based civil service system for government employment, and legislation regulating the political activity of federal employees.

When the Nixon administration took office in January 1969, it found just over 2,000 positions not previously locked into civil service to which the president could appoint individuals of his own choosing. To these posts, Mr. Nixon appointed approximately 70 percent Republicans and 20 percent Democrats. Roughly 10 percent of the positions were filled by either independents or persons with no known party affiliation.

Because of these changes, the who-you-know concept has come to relate less at the national level to government jobs—as any congressman will tell you who has tried to help a constituent obtain federal employment—and more to the subtleties of politics. These range from opened doors for big party contributors interested in obtaining government contracts, to sympathetic hearings for conglomerates defending themselves against antitrust charges, to high-level ambassadorial appointments.

At the local level, the same quid pro quo prevails, but sometimes in less subtle fashion. The chairman of the party controlling the county government may be instrumental in seeing that a close friend gets the insurance contract on the county's buildings. But, in turn, the insurance agent may be called upon to contribute to the party's war chest for the forthcoming campaign. The same applies to the employee who got his job with the help of his party connections. He may well be solicited to buy tickets to a party fund-raising dinner.

This pretty well confirms what I've always felt—that favoritism still plays a big part in politics.

Wherever the power exists to appoint, to award contracts, to prosecute, the stigma of favoritism goes with it. One of New York City's Tammany Hall leaders, Edward Costykian, put it this way: "The basic lesson I quickly learned was that a political leader cannot afford to insult his supporters by rewarding his opponents."

President Woodrow Wilson learned this from his postmaster general, Albert Burleson, who argued with Wilson about his refusal at first to permit political considerations to enter into appointments. Burleson warned that this position could jeopardize the president's programs with Congress, and added, "The little offices . . . are inconsequential . . . but they mean a great deal to the Senators and Representatives in Congress. If they are turned down, they will hate you and will not vote for anything you want. It is human nature." Wilson reconsidered and gave in.

These days, favoritism plays a lesser role in national politics than ever before. One reason is concern for this unwritten but overriding rule: that the action taken must be credible if questioned and defensible if exposed to public view. The company awarded a government contract must either have a proven record of performance or be able to deliver on the contract; the exercise of discretion by the Justice Department in whether or not to prosecute an antitrust case must carry with it reasonable grounds for the action taken; and the newly appointed ambassador not only must have adequate credentials for the job, but must be able to undergo close Senate scrutiny prior to confirmation.

I've heard politics defined as the "art of the possible." What does that mean?

The term means compromising not on what must be done but on what can be done. Chancellor Bismarck of Prussia is generally credited with authoring the quote when he defined politics as "the doctrine of the possible, the attainable."

Basically, the practical politician is a realist rather than a pure idealist, who works towards an objective, accepting conditions as they exist and people for what they are rather than for what he thinks they ought to be. He is prepared to take half a loaf when he knows a whole loaf is unattainable. That's the essence of politics.

How many public offices are there in this country to which politicians are elected?

By best count, close to one million. These include offices from the federal level down to the local school boards.

How many politicians are there in the country?

According to the latest edition of *Who's Who in American Politics*, there are approximately 16,000 key persons who make politics go in this country. In addition, there are roughly six million other citizens who are actively engaged in some form of political activity, from running for various offices to supporting and working for the parties or candidates of their choice.

The 16,000 key posts include the president of the United States, the vice-president, members of the cabinet, and other top presidential appointees in the administration; U.S. senators and representatives and their chief staff aides; governors, lieutenant governors, and their top administrative appointees; members of state legislatures; mayors and leading city councilmen; and key national, state, county, and local staff personnel of the major parties.

I hear a lot of complaining about politicians. Is this view widespread?

There are seeming contradictions in public attitudes about politicians. For example, in a 1971 Gallup Poll compilation of the ten men "most admired" by the American people, six are politicians, including five of the first six names on the list. President Nixon tops the list, followed by the Rev. Billy Graham, Sen. Edward M. Kennedy (D–Mass.), Lyndon B. Johnson, Sen. Hubert Humphrey (D–Minn.), Vice President Spiro Agnew, Ralph Nader, Pope Paul VI, Bob Hope and Alabama Governor George Wallace.

Another poll, conducted in 1972 by Louis Harris, reported both positive and negative attitudes toward politicians on the part of the American people. On the one hand, Harris found Americans by an 80 to 11 percent margin believe "most men go into elected office to help others." By 76 to 15 percent, they feel "most men in public life have little privacy and are often unfairly criticized" and by 55 to 26 percent, they go along with the view that "working in government as a career is one of the most useful and public spirited professions."

At the same time, Harris reported that distrust of politicians has risen in recent years. For instance, by an 81 to 11 percent margin, people agree with the statement that "most elected officials promise one thing at election time and do something different once in office." By 65 to 25 percent, they go along with the charge that "only a few men in politics are dedicated public servants." By 63 to 17 percent, they concur in the view that "most political jobs are not given on merit." And by 68 to 28 percent, they go along with the statement that "most politicians are in politics to make money for themselves."

Would you spell out the difference between a politician and a statesman?

David Lloyd George, the famed British prime minister who lived from 1863 to 1945, best defined the difference in these terms: "A politician is a person with whose politics you don't agree. If you agree with him, he is a statesman."

I've heard the phrase, "a statesman is a dead politician." Where did it come from and just what does it mean?

The quote originated from a well-known phrasemaker of the last century, Thomas Brackett Reed of Maine. In response to a written request in 1880 to define statesman, Reed, who later became Speaker of the U.S. House of Representatives, replied, "A statesman is a successful politician who is dead."

More recently, former President Harry S Truman used the phrase in a speech after leaving the White House. "A statesman is a politician who's been dead ten or fifteen years," said Truman.

The phrase has come to refer to a person who has risen to public prominence via elected politics and forgotten it was politics which put him there in the first place—in effect, writing off his base of political support and negating his chances for reelection. "He has become a statesman," is the derogatory phrase often used by professional politicians to describe someone whom they feel has "risen above politics."

What's meant by the term "power politics"? Where did it start?

The term "power politics" came into use in this country around the turn of the century, referring in the international sense to the concept that "might makes right." Today, it is used in the American political vocabulary in the context of running roughshod over the opposition.

What about the New Politics? Just what is it?

Largely developed and popularized by the newspapers and television in 1968, the term New Politics was at first ascribed to the youth-oriented, left-of-center movement aimed at reforming the establishment and correcting the nation's ills. Its chief coalescing point was the anti-Vietnam issue, and its membership, largely unorganized, came mainly from the campus and intellectual militants.

As American troop strength in Southeast Asia was reduced, the rallying point of the New Politics began to dissipate. At the same time, the movement shifted its emphasis from the streets to the voting booths, where its impact has yet to be measured. Today, the term New Politics has taken on another meaning—that of the use of sophisticated campaign techniques to elect candidates for office, including the employment of high-powered management teams, mass media, particularly television, and polling and computer services.

Critics of the new approach characterize it as "modern Madison Ave-

"CZAR" REED IS READY.

THE SPEAKER—I'M READY FOR THE FIFTY-SIXTH CONGRESS. SEE WHAT I DID TO THE FIFTY-FOURTH AND FIFTY-FIRST.

Speaker of the U.S. House of Representatives Thomas Brackett Reed of Maine —often called "Czar" Reed by his critics—prepares for the start of the Fifty-sixth Congress in this January 1899 drawing. Reed, who ran the House with a tough will, is credited with originating the phrase, "a statesman is a dead politician." *From the Collections of the Library of Congress.*

nue" which they say depersonalizes the candidate, establishes barriers between him and his constituency, and relegates the discussion of vital issues to a secondary role at best. Adherents of the new concept say it is nothing more than the updating and systemization of old techniques, which simply enables the candidate to project his best side to the voters at all times.

Okay, but is the New Politics really new?

Although the techniques and equipment are new, the concept isn't. Candidates from the beginning of the elective process have sought to pinpoint voters friendly to them and to put their best foot forward.

As far back as the 1840 presidential campaign, Abraham Lincoln, who was a member of a Whig committee for Illinois, spelled out this campaign plan in a memo to county committees:

> Our intention is to so organize the whole State so that every Whig can be brought to the polls. . . . Divide your county into small districts and appoint in each a subcommittee, whose duty shall be to make a perfect list of all voters . . . and ascertain with certainty for whom they will vote. . . . Keep a constant watch on the doubtful voters and . . . have them talked to by those in whom they have the most confidence. . . . On election day, see that every Whig is brought to the polls.

Today, campaign management teams, electronic computers, and opinion polls do much the same job.

The effort by candidates to project the best image of themselves to voters isn't new either. Back in 1927, philosopher John Dewey, commenting on the campaigns of his day, declared, "The tidal waves swamp some [candidates], the landslide carries others into offices. Habit, party funds, skills of managers of the machine, the portrait of the candidate with his firm jaw, his lovely wife and children, and a multitude of other irrelevancies determine the issue." Except for the injection of modern technology, the campaigns of Mr. Lincoln's and Mr. Dewey's day sound a lot like today's New Politics.

I hear a lot about machine politics. What's the difference between a machine and an organization?

A quick answer is that a machine belongs to the opposition; an organization is yours. Actually, of course, there is more to it than that. The term "machine" generally refers to a well-disciplined group, usually operating under a boss or leader, whose objectives are to elect its own officials and secure itself in power. The term "organization" usually suggests higher motives and objectives, although organizations may tend to become machines once they "throw the rascals out" and take over themselves.

In his excellent work, *The New Language of Politics*, William Safire noted, "To the reformer, the machine is dominated by a 'boss' and consists of his 'henchmen' and 'dupes'; to a regular, the organization is headed by a 'leader' and consists of 'activists' and 'public-spirited citizens.'"

Just what is a political boss? Are bosses still running politics in this country?

A political boss is a leader who effectively controls the party machinery in his area. Although he may not be an elected public official, he nevertheless exerts wide power over those in his party who are elected.

Political bosses and bossism first came into public prominence after the Civil War, when the nation's economic base began to shift from agriculture to industry. Along with an amazing growth in the city populations came a comparable expansion in political party organizations to minister to the masses who needed help in finding jobs, places to live, food to eat, or simply recognition of their worth as human beings—all in exchange for their votes on election day.

The word "boss" evolved from the New York Dutch who had a similar term, *baas*, which by conversion over a period of time became boss.

Although William Marcy Tweed of New York City, who came into control of Tammany Hall in the 1860s, was the most widely known of U.S. political bosses, he wasn't the first. In fact, political bossism in some form is as old as politics in this country, predating the Revolutionary War. For instance, John Adams' diary, which was published in 1850, carried this entry for February of 1763:

> This day learned that the Caucus Club meets at certain times in the garret of Tom Dawes, the Adjutant of the Boston Regiment. He has a large house and he has a movable partition in his garret which he takes down and the whole club meets in one room. There they smoke tobacco til you cannot see from one end of the garret to the other. There they drink flip, I suppose, and they choose a moderator who puts questions to the vote regularly. . . . Selectmen, assessors, collectors, fire-wards, and representatives are regularly chosen before they are chosen in the town.

Although bossism has existed in some form in this country for as long as politics has, it has changed markedly from the old style practiced by Boss Tweed and others like him. One of the reasons for the erosion of bossism is an expanded federal government role in state and local affairs which has weakened local control over everything from federal patronage (replacing it with the civil service system) to social-welfare programs (substituting for them federal unemployment insurance, workman's compensation, Social Security, Medicare, etc.). Another factor is the increase in the material security of the workingman, with fewer Americans economically deprived these days.

In short, with a few scattered exceptions here and there across the country, such as Mayor Richard Daley of Chicago, old-style bossism has largely declined. And the elements which thrust them onto the American political scene have largely disappeared as well.

You mentioned Tammany Hall earlier. Just what is it?

Tammany Hall, headquarters for the political organization which controlled New York City's Democratic party for nearly a century, drew its name from the Society of Tammany, founded in the late eighteenth century as a "defender of democracy." The society's name came from a renowned Delaware Indian chief. With the help of such political leaders as Aaron Burr, the organization moved into active control of the party and established what came to symbolize the worst in big-city machine politics. Today, like most such machines, it is in a state of disrepair.

How did the word "caucus" get started?

A caucus is a closed-door meeting of a political party or group. The origin is believed to have been the name of a club which existed in Boston in the eighteenth century, "West Corcus." Another story has it that the term derives from an Algonquin Indian word "caucauasu," which meant elder or counselor or one who advises. There are still other explanations, none of which seems to have more credibility than these.

The term "carpetbagger" is sometimes used in political campaigns. Just where did it originate?

The term comes from the suitcases or carryall bags made of carpet material which travelers used extensively in the last century. It came into wide usage after the Civil War in reference to northerners who moved

south to obtain political offices or influence by catering to the newly enfranchised black voters.

Today, the term is still used, primarily in a derogatory sense, against
a stranger who moves into a new area to seek political gain or to run for
office.

I've been hearing a lot about the new "Populism." Just what is it?

A resurrection of sorts of the "anti-big-interests" tenets of the short-
lived Populist party which was founded in 1891, the new version echoes
the concern for the little guy, the average American, that the original did.

Its theme in the seventies is attention to what the plain people, as
contrasted with the rich and educated, need and think. Alabama Governor
George C. Wallace has been one of the most consistent examples of the
revival which has forced other national political figures to ape it, at least
in token fashion. In an exhaustive piece in the *Washington Post* on May
7, 1972, before the attempted assassination of Wallace, reporter William
Greider captured the essential Wallace as a presidential primary candidate:

> Wallace never gives a speech without cataloguing that list of big
> guys who are against him. His voice is authentic, a genuine mix of
> the anger, nostalgia and resentment which the originals evoked. When
> Wallace denounces welfare free-loaders, he remembers his own hard
> times as a boy:
> "I lived in a house with no indoor plumbing. . . . I didn't have
> any lamplight. We had to draw water. I couldn't get a dollar cowboy
> suit out of Sears Roebuck because we didn't have the dollar. So I
> know what it was to be poor. We were good folks and we were proud
> people, but we didn't have much."

Greider also cited another variation called "stylistic populism": "What
the candidate must get across is that he is unslick, unrich, unprofessional,
unestablishment. Issues . . . are important only as vehicles to express this."

In one of the early instances of its appearance in the second half of
the twentieth century, the term "populist" was used to describe President
Lyndon Johnson during his tenure in office as someone "in the old populist
tradition." Another excellent example was the 1968 reelection campaign
slogan of Washington Senator Warren Magnuson—"Keep the Big Boys
Honest."

I've heard so much about the so-called Eastern Establishment. Just what is it?

The Eastern Establishment, also known as the Eastern Liberal Establishment, is a loose-knit mixture of financial, banking, legal, and communications interests headquartered for the most part in New York City. Educated chiefly at boarding schools and Ivy League colleges and trained in the professions of their fathers, the Establishment men move easily and comfortably at those intersections of national life where Wall Street, Madison, and Pennsylvania Avenues come together.

Although generally liberal Republican in politics, the Eastern Establishment has provided men for high government posts of both major parties. Sometimes called "kingmakers" in the context of U.S. presidential politics, the Establishment has influenced the nomination of just about every Republican candidate from 1936 until 1960, when Richard Nixon was nominated with the Establishment bowing to the inevitable. In 1964, Barry Goldwater's nomination was secured over the opposition of the Establishment which was outmanned and outmaneuvered. Since then, the Establishment has fallen into some disrepair, with its principals split in 1968 between the nomination of New York's Governor Nelson Rockefeller and Nixon. The defection from the GOP of the Establishment's mayor of New York City, John Lindsay, has contributed to the state in which it now finds itself.

Is there also a Conservative Establishment in America?

Yes, but it's not as well known as the Eastern or Liberal Establishment nor nearly as strategically located. Its power base is largely the business community and the professions, plus large areas of rural and small-town America. Geographically, it cuts across regions of the country. Such powerful organizations as the U.S. Chamber of Commerce, the National Association of Manufacturers, the American Medical Association, the Farm Bureau, and the American Legion are the backbone of the Conservative Establishment.

Where did the terms "conservative" and "liberal" come from?

Although its usage can be traced back in some form or another to the eighteenth century in France and the nineteenth century in England, use of the word "conservative" in this country grew out of the term "Tory," which was applied to Americans who remained loyal to King George III during the Revolutionary War. Because Tory was considered an objectionable word in the United States in those days, it was superceded in the early 1800s by the label "conservative." In fact, Tory as a political party name was dropped in Great Britain in 1830 and replaced by Conservative, which gave stimulus to its further usage in this country.

One of the early written U.S. references to the word was in 1837 when it was applied to Democrats who opposed President Martin Van Buren's subtreasury plan. Former President John Quincy Adams, the only former chief executive to be elected to the U.S. House after leaving the White House, wrote in his diary on October 11, 1837, that Rep. James M. Mason of Virginia spoke "for the party called the Conservative." Three days later, Adams referred in his diary to Rep. John C. Clark as "one of the New York Conservatives, as they are now called."

Conservative was later applied to congressional Republicans who opposed the harsh reconstruction program against the South of the so-called Radical Republicans after the Civil War. Some southern Democrats who shared this opposition were also branded as conservatives, a label which came to reflect the political philosophy of most southerners in Congress from that time to the present.

The term "liberal" was first used in France and England in the early 1800s to describe opponents of the aristocratic form of government in those countries. The liberal of those days was someone who opposed government encroachment on individual liberties.

One of the first references to the term in this country was in Congressman Adams' diary on January 17, 1838, when he noted in connection with a resolution before the House of Representatives that "the usual debate between the economists and the liberals, commenced yesterday, was now continued, till the expiration of the hour."

Years later, in 1872, a fragment of the Republican party calling itself the Liberal Republican party was organized to fight the renomination of President Ulysses S. Grant, whose patronage abuses and reconstruction policies they opposed. The group met in convention at Cincinnati on May 1, nominated Horace Greeley for president and B. Gratz Brown for vice-president, and adopted a platform endorsing civil service reforms, states' rights, reconciliation with the South, and full-scale amnesty for former Confederates. The Democratic National Convention meeting that year at Philadelphia endorsed the Liberal Republican slate and its platform—the first and last time the Democratic party failed to nominate its own candidates for president and vice-president.

Although the Liberal Republicans started out as a third-party movement, they immediately became one of the two major parties with the endorsement by the Democratic convention. But the Greeley–Brown candidacy fragmented the Democratic party so badly that the better-organized and funded Republican forces swept Grant back into office with 3.6 million votes to Greeley's 2.8 million, the biggest defeat for a presidential candidate up to that time. The sadly disappointed Greeley, whose wife had died just before the election, suffered a physical and mental breakdown and died on November 29, less than a month after his crushing defeat. The Liberal Republican party which he helped to found failed to survive Greeley's loss and died itself soon thereafter.

Although the term "liberal" was little used in the latter part of the nineteenth and early part of the twentieth centuries, it came back into popular usage during the 1920s and later during the presidency of Franklin D. Roosevelt (1933–1945) who used it frequently to describe his administration and programs.

One of the best light summations of the differences between a conservative and a liberal came from the American short-story writer and journalist, Ambrose Bierce, who put it this way: "A conservative is one enamoured of existing evils, as distinguished from the liberal who wishes to replace them with others."

I've heard it said that "liberal" and "conservative" have lost most of their original meaning and are useless today as political labels. Is this true?

In one sense, yes. The terms have become so overused and misused to label people, programs, and philosophies that many politicians shy away from them. One problem is that the guidelines change over the years so that what may have been considered liberal twenty years ago is today considered acceptable by the conservatives, and vice versa. For instance, Medicare, once opposed by conservatives, is today accepted by them; law and order, once labeled by some liberals as a "code word" for racism, is today part of the liberal as well as the conservative dogma. In short, conservative politicians would no more run against Medicare today than the liberals would against law and order.

When the word conservative is used these days, it is usually to describe someone who believes the private sector can better meet the pressing problems facing the country than the government, and that when it can't, state and local action is preferable to federal action. He also prefers the tried and tested over the untried and experimental. Contrary to some definitions, most conservatives claim they aren't against change but believe it must come slowly and only after irrefutable demonstration of need—and then only within the framework of the existing system and institutions.

When the word liberal is used these days, it usually refers to someone who believes in a philosophy of government in which the solution to pressing problems can be best achieved by more government action and programs rather than less.

Unlike the conservative, the liberal believes change must come quickly and in pace with changing conditions, and for this reason he is willing to experiment with the untried in hopes of effecting rapid solutions. If necessary, the liberal believes in changing the institutions themselves.

Where did the terms "right" and "left" originate? What do they mean today?

The two terms came from the designations of political factions in the French National Assembly in the eighteenth century. The monarchists and conservative nobles sat to the presiding officer's right, the moderates in the center, directly in front of him, and the radicals to his left. From this arrangement, right, center, and left came to mean conservative, moderate, and liberal.

Today, the terms are usually used in this country to refer to the wings or factions within the two major political parties rather than to the parties themselves. Interestingly, although the GOP is the more conservative of the two parties, Republicans sit to the presiding officer's left in the U.S. Senate and the U.S. House of Representatives, and the Democrats to his right.

What about the political center? Just where is it located?

It's located right where you'd expect it to be—in the middle between the Right and the Left—the middle of the road, as it is often called. According to a 1972 poll by Louis Harris, more Americans consider themselves to be middle-of-the-roaders (35 percent) than either liberal (19 percent) or conservative (29 percent). In fact, only 4 percent of the voters classify themselves as radical. The remaining 13 percent were unsure.

Because of the large centrist viewpoint in this country, candidates for public office seek to shift away from positions reflecting extremism and toward the political center. Richard M. Scammon and Ben J. Wattenberg, writing in their excellent book, *The Real Majority*, predict that "the struggle to capture the center in the 1970s . . . will determine who will be the next presidents."

What is the lunatic fringe?

Essentially, it is the extremist element at either end of the political spectrum. Theodore Roosevelt is credited with first using the term in a letter to Sen. Henry Cabot Lodge in February 1913, four months after Roosevelt was defeated as the Progressive party's presidential candidate. "The various admirable movements in which I have been engaged have always developed among their members a large lunatic fringe," Roosevelt said. Later, in his autobiography, he declared, "There is a lunatic fringe to every reform movement."

The term has since become a part of our political vocabulary to label in a derogatory way militant movements of the far Right and far Left.

How about the statement that "politics makes strange bedfellows"? How did it originate and what does it mean?

The original source most likely was Shakespeare in *The Tempest*. In that play, the jester, Trinculo, seeks shelter from a sudden storm under a gaberdine sheet with the monster Caliban. Comments Trinculo, "Misery acquaints a man with strange bedfellows."

The phrase was picked up by Charles Dudley Warner, editor of the Hartford (Connecticut) *Courant*, who wrote in 1850, "True it is that politics makes strange bedfellows." Warner later used the same phrase in his *My Summer in a Garden*, published in 1870.

In essence, the phrase suggests an uneasy or unexpected alliance of enemies or unlikes who are forced by circumstances to cooperate or work together. A recent example was the Kennedy–Johnson ticket in 1960 in which John F. Kennedy, liberal, urbane, and Harvard-educated, asked Lyndon B. Johnson, conservative, Texas-born, and pragmatic, to be his vice-presidential running mate.

I'm confused—are we living in a republic or a democracy? What's the difference, really?

By usage over the years, these two terms have become somewhat inter-changeable. Both are now used to convey the idea of a government in which the people exercise power through their elected representatives.

Strictly speaking, the U.S. government is a republic and not a democracy. The distinction is that, in a republic, the people elect public officials to act as their representatives in the councils of government. In a democ-

racy, the people assemble and conduct the business of government themselves. Because of the size of the United States, spreading over some 3.6
million square miles, and its population which is now well over 200 million,
the business of the American government must be conducted through
elected representatives.

The word "republic" is derived from the Latin *res publica*, which
means public thing or affair. "Democracy" is derived from the Greek
demos, which means people, and *kratein*, meaning to rule.

When the delegates to the Constitutional Convention met in Philadelphia to decide which type of government the United States should
have, a woman stopped Benjamin Franklin as he left the convention hall
to ask, "Well, what have we got—a republic or a monarchy?" Franklin
replied, "A republic, if you can keep it." A democracy in its pure sense
was unthinkable to the colonists at that time.

**Set me straight on something else. Is there basically any difference between
socialism and communism?**

Although there are similarities, there are also differences. The word
"socialism" derives from the Latin *socius*, which means sharing in. Communism stems from the Latin *communus*, meaning common.

To oversimplify, socialists generally advocate public ownership of major
national resources, general utilities, and the means of production in a
country. Communists advocate public ownership of all property. Socialists
generally advocate adoption of their system by peaceful and legal means,
while communists advocate the use of revolutionary methods. As the
terms are used these days, all communists are socialists but not all socialists
are communists. G. W. Gough described the difference in his 1926 book,
The Economic Consequences of Socialism, this way: "The Communist
is a Socialist in a violent hurry."

I still hear the word McCarthyism bandied about. Would you define it?

The term, which obtained its name from the late Sen. Joseph R. Mc-
Carthy of Wisconsin, was used chiefly by his critics to describe his free-
wheeling allegations of Communists in government in the early 1950s,
and his widespread public charges against people he suspected of Communist connections.

On the one hand, McCarthy's opponents claimed that his techniques
and charges were irresponsible and inadequately documented, a threat to
individual liberty in this country and to the orderly conduct of govern-

ment. Conversely, his supporters believed McCarthy to be a highly motivated patriot who had succeeded in alerting the nation to the dangers of internal subversion. In the end, McCarthy's own excesses brought on a vote of censure against him by his Senate colleagues on December 2, 1954. His power curtailed, he dropped from the limelight and died in 1957.

Today, the term McCarthyism has become part of the American political vocabulary, used to describe (1) the employment of well-publicized, but sometimes inadequately documented, charges against public figures, or (2) an official investigation which fails to provide proper safeguards for the rights of the individuals under investigation.

Senator McCarthy often accused people of being "fellow travellers." Where did the term originate and just what does it mean?

Although the term was used by Senator McCarthy in the early 1950s to describe persons whom he believed were allied in some way with the Communist party, sympathizing with its aims and accepting its doctrines, it has also taken on the broader definition of one who believes in the policies of an organization or party without actually joining or publicly working for it.

The phrase is Old English in origin, used in those days to describe a travelling companion going the same way. It was also used by the Russians with varied meanings. Writing in *The Nation* in 1936, Max Lerner said, "The term has a Russian background and means someone who does not accept all of your aims but has enough in common with you to accompany you in a comradely fashion part of the way."

Where did the term "demagogue" come from?

Originating from the Greek word *demagogos*, which means one who leads the people, the term was first applied in ancient Greece to an orator or leader who sided with the people over the state. Since many of these so-called leaders were proven wrong, the term took on the meaning of one who misled the people.

Today, although the word is often bandied about recklessly, it has come to mean, in its mildest sense, a politician who tells the people what he thinks they want to hear rather than what they ought to hear. In its severest description, it means an unprincipled opportunist who panders to the fears, passions, and prejudices of the people rather than to their intelligence.

How about the terms "hawk" and "dove"? How did they originate?

The term "hawk" dates back to the immediate post-Revolutionary War days in this country. Coined by Thomas Jefferson in 1798, it was applied to certain Federalist "war hawks" whom he charged were trying to press the United States into war with France. Later, in 1811, the label was attached to members of Congress who advocated war with Great Britain in hopes of expanding U.S. territory. By the following year, 1812, the war hawks had forced the hand of President Madison and the United States was at war with Britain—without question the least successful of American wars until Vietnam.

The term "dove" derives from the ancient Greek goddess of love, Aphrodite, who had a dove perched on her arm symbolizing peace and tranquillity.

The two terms surfaced early in the Vietnam war. Generally, hawk was used to describe advocates of strong military action against North Vietnam, aimed at achieving victory. Dove was used to designate either advocates of an immediate disengagement of U.S. troops from that country or of the establishment of a deadline for such disengagement.

Where did the term "silent majority" come from? Who first used it?

"Silent majority" in its current usage was first employed by President Nixon on November 3, 1969, in a nationally televised address on the Vietnam war. Outlining his plan for ending the war and bringing home U.S. troops, the president concluded by saying, "And so tonight—to you, the great silent majority of my fellow Americans—I ask your support."

Basically, the term is an updated version of the "forgotten man" employed in the last century by William Graham Sumner, professor of political science at Yale University. In 1883, Sumner delivered a lecture at Yale in which he discussed the forgotten man in these terms:

> Wealth comes only from production—and all that the wrangling grabbers, loafers and jobbers get to deal with comes from somebody's toil and sacrifice. Who then is he who provides it all? The Forgotten Man . . . delving away in patient industry, supporting his family, paying his taxes, casting his vote, supporting the church and school . . . . Such is the Forgotten Man. He works, he votes, generally he prays, but his chief business in life is to pay and he always pays. All burdens fall on him. . . .

Although Sumner had used the phrase to describe the solid citizen of his day, Walter Hines Page used it in a speech at the North Carolina Teachers' College in Raleigh in 1897 to define the average man. Later, New York's Governor Franklin D. Roosevelt picked up the concept and used it in his 1932 campaign for the presidency, in the sense of the under-privileged man or the underdog.

In another context, "The Silent Majority" was used in the *New Harper's Monthly* magazine of September 1874, as a headline over an article dealing with the dead.

CHAPTER 2

Are political parties necessary?

How many political parties are there in the United States?

Altogether, about 35. The two major ones, of course, are the Democratic and Republican parties. The rest are mostly local in nature, with some operating in just one state or city.

The only party in addition to the Republicans and Democrats to qualify for inclusion on the ballots of each of the 50 states in recent years was the American Independent party (AIP) headed by Alabama Governor George C. Wallace in 1968.

Other minor parties include the Liberal party, Conservative party, American party, Constitutional Union party, National party, Peace and Freedom party, Prohibition party, Socialist Labor party, and the Socialist Workers party.

How did the two-party system in this country get started?

Prior to 1790, the United States had no formally organized parties to which voters could give their support. The two loose coalitions at the time consisted of (1) the Federalists, who believed in a strong central government, loose construction of the Constitution, and who supported the administrations of George Washington and John Adams, and (2) the Anti-Federalists, who later became known as the Republicans, and who believed in states' rights, strict construction of the Constitution, and who opposed the Washington and Adams administrations.

President Washington, although sometimes referred to as a Federalist, regarded himself as nonpartisan and tried to steer a middle course between the two groups. In fact, the framers of the Constitution had not considered the possibility of powerful political parties developing in this country and Washington himself had warned the American people in his Farewell Address against the dangers of dividing into parties.

Nevertheless, two distinct parties began to emerge about 1790, with one, the Anti-Federalist Republicans, coalescing around the leadership of Thomas Jefferson, then secretary of state, and the other, the Federalists, around Alexander Hamilton, then secretary of the treasury. Although Jefferson and his followers usually referred to themselves as Republicans, they were sometimes called Democratic–Republicans, a hyphenation they sought to discard after the name Democratic became unpopular because of the excesses of the French revolutionists who were known as *Democrats.*

Although no formal party nominations were made for president in the elections of 1796, it was understood that Jefferson was the Republican candidate and Adams the Federalist candidate. Adams received seventy-one electoral votes to Jefferson's sixty-eight, with 137 scattered among eleven other men. This made Adams president and Jefferson vice-president under provisions of the Constitution as it then stood.

Because electors were not pledged in advance in those days to vote for a particular candidate, several from states which Jefferson carried switched to Adams. This decided the Republicans in the election of 1800 to put up their own lists of electors, in what was really the beginning of the two-party system in this country.

Which of the two parties today is the older? How was it started?

In the sense of today's parties, the Democrats are the older of the two. After Thomas Jefferson was elected president in 1800, the hyphenated Democratic–Republican label came back into prominence, with some members of the party dropping the word Republican. In the presidential elections of 1804 through 1816, Federalist candidates were overwhelmingly defeated by Democratic–Republican candidates, and the Federalists, as an organized entity, dropped out of sight shortly thereafter.

In the election of 1824, there were four candidates for president, all members of the same party which by then was called by three names—

The first Democratic president was Andrew Jackson, who ran under the loose banner of that party in 1828 and was elected over the incumbent, John Quincy Adams. Jackson was renominated in 1832 at the Democrats' first formal convention. Since then, the party of Jackson has become known officially as the Democratic party. *From the Collections of the Library of Congress.*

Republican, Democratic–Republican, and Democratic. None of the four received a majority of the electoral votes, and John Quincy Adams was chosen by the House of Representatives. Andrew Jackson, one of the three losers, decided to challenge Adams in the 1828 elections and soundly defeated him. President Jackson's supporters, regarding themselves as the true heirs of Jefferson, gradually weaned the party name away from the hyphenated Democratic–Republican to just Democratic. In fact, the first Democratic National Convention was held in 1832, four years after Jackson's election, and proceeded to renominate him for the presidency.

From then on, there was no question about it—the party of Jackson was the Democratic party, which has elected twelve presidents, and has controlled the government for seventy-two of the 144 years since its founding.

How did the Republican party get started?

Although there's some dispute over just when and where the Republican party was born, the movement that led to its formation was set off by the passage in 1854 of the Kansas–Nebraska bill which permitted slavery in territory that had been previously free. Even before the bill was passed by Congress, a loose coalition of antislavery Whigs, Democrats, Abolitionists, and Free Soilers met at a schoolhouse at Ripon, Wisconsin, on March 20, 1854, and resolved, if the bill became law, "to throw old party organizations to the winds and organize a new party on the sole basis of the non-extension of slavery."

Although a small frame building on the Ripon College campus is claimed with some validity as the birthplace of the Republican party, the formal organization of the party did not take place until later, on July 6, 1854, in Jackson, Michigan, where several thousand delegates met outdoors under the oaks because there wasn't a hall large enough to accommodate them. They went on record against the Kansas–Nebraska bill and formally organized a new party to be named Republican.

Although Republican had been discussed prior to the Jackson meeting as a possible name for the party, credit for initially urging its adoption usually goes to A. E. Bovay, a young lawyer who had helped organize the March 20 Ripon meeting. He spelled out his suggestions in letters to Horace Greeley, editor of the *New York Tribune*, in February and again in June of 1854. The formal adoption of the name, however, was at the Jackson meeting on July 6 of that year.

Launched largely by nonprofessionals, the new party did not at first have a leader of national stature. It was simply a loose-knit series of state

GOP birthplace? At this small schoolhouse in Ripon, Wisconsin, a loose coalition of antislavery Whigs, Democrats, Abolitionists, and Free Soilers met on March 20, 1854, and founded what was later called the Republican party.

The first Republican presidential candidate was John C. Fremont, who was nominated by the newly organized party in 1854 at its convention in Philadelphia. Fremont's running mate was William L. Dayton of New Jersey. Although the Fremont-Dayton ticket wasn't elected, it polled enough votes to assure the GOP a major role in the future. Its candidate four years later was Abraham Lincoln. *From a painting at the University of Michigan Museum of Art.*

parties without central organization of any kind. This was rectified at a meeting in Pittsburgh on February 22, 1856, called by the state Republican committees of Pennsylvania, Ohio, Massachusetts, Wisconsin, Michigan, and Vermont. The Pittsburgh meeting ratified Republican as the official name for the party, set up a national committee, and laid plans to hold a presidential nominating convention later in the year.

The new party held its first national convention in Philadelphia on June 17, 1856. It went on record against slavery, against polygamy, and in favor of the principles of Washington and Jefferson, federal aid to the Pacific railroad, and the use of federal funds to improve the nation's rivers and harbors.

The convention nominated John C. Fremont, "the Pathfinder of the West," for president and William L. Dayton of New Jersey for vice-president. Abraham Lincoln, who had just joined the new party, received 110 votes for vice-president. Although the Fremont–Dayton ticket did not win, the two Republican candidates carried sufficient electoral and popular votes to assure the new party a major political role in the future.

Writing in the *New York Tribune* on July 9, 1859, Horace Greeley commented, "The Republican Party . . . was called into being solely to resist the encroachments of slavery upon the free territory of the Union and upon the free states. It was a combination of men of varying political antecedents; some had been Whigs, some Democrats, some Americans, some Abolitionists, some had always kept aloof from politics."

From those beginnings, the Republican party, which had started out as a one-issue third party, became two years later a second party and four years after that elected its first president, Abraham Lincoln. It then held the reins of government for the next twenty years without interruption. Altogether, since its founding 118 years ago, the Republican party has elected fourteen presidents and controlled the government for sixty-eight years.

How did the Republican party get its nickname, GOP?

The initials stand for Grand Old Party. Although its origin has become somewhat obscured by time, the early uses of the term came in Congress—interestingly, in reference to the Democratic party. But the term was gradually shifted over to apply to the Republican party, particularly by newspapers which found GOP easier to fit into headlines or into editorial cartoons than the much longer Republican party. After the term began to catch on, the Democrats took it up in derision, but, by so doing, helped cement it into the U.S. political vocabulary as an abbreviation for the Republican party.

How about the elephant and donkey symbols for the two parties? How did they come about?

Both were popularized as party symbols by cartoonist Thomas Nast in *Harper's Weekly*. He first used the donkey to symbolize the Democratic party in a cartoon in the January 15, 1870, issue of the publication and the elephant to signify the Republican party nearly five years later, in the November 7, 1874, issue.

Although Nast is generally credited with the creation of the donkey and elephant symbols, there is substantial evidence that both had been used earlier. For instance, one of the Abraham Lincoln banners paraded at the Republican National Convention of 1860 had an elephant imprinted on it. The *Field Piece*, a Whig campaign publication, printed a woodcut on July 19, 1848, showing a donkey which was labeled the "Democratic platform." Even earlier, Democratic President Martin Van Buren was needled in an 1837 cartoon in which a donkey was used to depict his party.

When did political parties start adopting platforms? Do platforms really mean anything?

The term "platform" originated from the French *plateforme*, which meant, literally, a plane or flat area and, figuratively, a chart or blueprint or plan of action. Its usage can be traced back to the sixteenth century in Europe.

In the United States, party platforms came into common usage about the same time as national nominating conventions. The Anti-Mason party led the way, adopting what has been labeled the first written platform of a national political party at its first nominating convention in 1831. The first Democratic convention a year later also adopted a platform of sorts, and the process became an accepted and expected part of each party's political ritual every four years.

In a practical sense, platforms provide guideposts for the voters as to party thinking on major issues and markers to which party members can point. Platforms frequently become a major source of controversy at the national conventions, and delegations have been known to walk out following the adoption of certain planks with which they strongly disagreed.

As far as the party's presidential candidate is concerned, even though

The Republican elephant came into popular usage as that party's symbol after the above cartoon by Thomas Nast was published in the November 7, 1874, issue of *Harper's Weekly*. Nast, who lived from 1840 to 1902, was the leading political cartoonist of his day. *From the Collections of the Library of Congress.*

Although Thomas Nast is credited with creating and popularizing the elephant as the symbol of the GOP and the donkey as the Democrats' symbol, there is some evidence of earlier usage of both animals to depict the two parties. This cartoon was first used in 1837 needling Democratic President Martin Van Buren and his party. *From the Collections of the Library of Congress.*

he usually tells convention delegates that he accepts "your nomination and your platform," for practical purposes he sets the party line for the remainder of the campaign and, if elected, for his tenure in the White House. Ordinarily, however, his views are reasonably in line with his party's platform.

"A LIVE JACKASS KICKING A DEAD LION."

And such a Lion! and such a Jackass!

The donkey came into its own as the Democratic party symbol with the publication of this Thomas Nast cartoon in the January 15, 1870, issue of *Harper's Weekly*. Although the animal in this cartoon is tied in specifically with the "Copperheads," northern Democrats who sympathized with the South, Nast soon began using the donkey to identify the party itself. *From the Collections of the Library of Congress.*

What I'm getting at is this—do the political parties follow through on their platform pledges?

Actually, yes. In a study of the parties' fulfillment of platform pledges between 1944 and 1966, Gerald M. Pomper reported in *Elections in America* that there was a high level of follow-through on these commitments. His study covered "testable" pledges in which results could be

Party platforms came into being about the same time as national nominating conventions, providing a base on which presidential candidates could run for election. The Democratic platform of 1856 illustrated above is the one on which James Buchanan ran and defeated John C. Fremont, the first Republican presidential candidate. Interestingly, one study shows that the two parties make good on 72 percent of their platform commitments. *From the Collections of the Library of Congress.*

measured in such areas as legislative action, presidential or other executive action, indirect action in which substantially similar activity to that promised was taken, and "negative fulfillment" in which a pledge was made not to act or to oppose action.

Out of nearly 1,400 testable pledges during this period, Pomper found that 72 percent had been fulfilled by the two parties, 18 percent had been defeated and 10 percent had no action at all taken. Bipartisan pledges—those contained in both parties' platforms—had the highest level of fulfillment with 85 percent, Pomper reported. In addition, the party which won the presidency had a better record of fulfillment than the out-party—with 79 percent of its pledges met against 53 percent for the out-party.

Which of the two parties had the best follow-through record on its platform pledges?

Although it's not too meaningful, Pomper found the Democrats had a fulfillment level of 68 percent compared to 62 percent for the Republicans. The reason this statistic isn't too significant is that the Democrats controlled Congress for eighteen of those twenty-two years, and the Presidency for fourteen of those years. The fulfillment opportunities of the party in charge of the White House and the Congress are always higher than those of the out-party.

I've heard it said that there's not "a dime's worth of difference" between the two major political parties. Is this true?

Although party platforms and programs often overlap and sometimes duplicate each other, there are several basic differences in the philosophies of each party and in their approach to government. Oversimplified, these differences boil down to the following:

1. The Republican party contends that the concentration of power in the national government in Washington should be avoided, wherever possible, and that the states and local governments closer to the people should be assigned the first tasks of governing. The Democratic party, conversely, holds that a strong national government is needed to deal with today's problems, which it feels are often too complex and costly for states or local governments to handle effectively.

2. The Republican party feels that unfettered private enterprise is a

force for growth and prosperity and should be regulated no more than neceessary to protect the public interest. The Democratic party's view is that the federal government should effect whatever regulation is needed to assure an adequate and expanding level of economic activity.

3. The Republican party contends that both management and labor are able to bargain from positions of approximately equal strength and that the government should intervene only when the public welfare is involved. The Democratic party feels that the government should at times throw its weight in various ways on the side of labor, in the belief that labor is at a disadvantage in dealing with management.

These basic differences in philosophy are reflected in many ways—in presidential decisions and appointments, in rulings by federal regulatory agencies, in nominations to the U.S. Supreme Court, and in Congress itself where the lawmakers split on a party line basis on roll-call votes close to 40 percent of the time. In fact, some of the major issues before Congress have been decided on a partisan basis, such as housing legislation, trade expansion laws, antipoverty programs, and Supreme Court appointments—all reflecting either the differing philosophies of the parties or support by party loyalists for legislation asked for by their man in the White House.

Although President Nixon frequently has veered outside his party's philosophical boundaries, he has nevertheless made numerous efforts to keep within them. For example, in an effort to reduce Washington's role, he has pressed for programs to turn back federal tax revenues to state and local governments to use on projects as they see fit. In another area, his appointees to such regulatory agencies as the National Labor Relations Board have reversed the thrust of prolabor board decisions under Democratic administrations.

Politics-watchers Scammon and Wattenberg sum it up: "Within the center, the two parties do stand for differing political philosophies: the Republicans are basically right of center; the Democrats basically left of center. The party that looks to Haynsworth and Carswell for the Supreme Court is not the ideological twin of the party that chooses Fortas and Thurgood Marshall."

Aside from these basic differences, which are also usually reflected in the platforms, the presidential candidates of the two major parties in an election are ordinarily not too far apart on issues of public policy. The most recent exception to this was the 1972 Nixon–McGovern campaign. More often than not, however, presidential campaigns come down to an argument over which of the candidates is better qualified to occupy the White House and which can best handle the nation's problems.

How about party differences at other levels, such as in Congress?

It's at the congressional level that the party differences show up most markedly. Although both parties contain members whose views span the political spectrum, Republicans in the Senate and House tend on the average to be middle to right of center while Democrats tend toward the middle and left-of-center area on major issues.

For instance, the Americans for Democratic Action (ADA), an organization which rates members of the Senate and House on their liberalism on key bills it selects, reported that in the two sessions of the Ninety-first Congress (1969–1970) Senate Republicans voted liberal an average of 31 percent of the time, compared with 57 percent for Democratic members. In the House, ADA rated Republican members as liberal 20 percent of the time and Democrats 50 percent.

Conversely, the Americans for Constitutional Action (ACA), an organization which assesses the conservatism of congressional members, rated Senate Republicans as voting conservative 60 percent and Democrats 32 percent. In the House, the same ratios generally applied, with ACA rating Republican members as 65 percent conservative on the average and Democrats as 33 percent.

How is party policy actually established at the national level?

In the case of the party controlling the White House, it is established primarily by the president and generally supported by party members in Congress and at state and local levels. However, disagreements do occur from time to time over specific policies.

When a party doesn't control the White House, policy is either set by its leaders in Congress—usually operating through their policy-making committees or caucuses in the Senate and House—or through broader-based coordinating committees or advisory committees. Membership on such committees ordinarily is drawn from all segments of the party and includes the most prominent names available, including former presidents or presidential candidates, governors, members of Congress, and former cabinet officers. Both the Republican and Democratic parties have employed these policy-forming committees in the past with varying degrees of success.

How long have the two parties had national committees?

Before the Democrats and Republicans began to operate on an organized basis, the various political parties in the early days of the country did not have permanent national committees. Several of these early parties set up what they called "committees of correspondence" each election year, which were dissolved immediately after the election.

The Democratic National Convention of 1848, however, established the first party national committee as a permanent organization and named B. P. Hallett of Massachusetts as the first chairman. There have been thirty-three chairmen since Hallett.

The Republican National Convention of 1856 ratified the establishment of a permanent Republican National Committee which had been agreed upon earlier in the year at an organization meeting of party leaders in Pittsburgh in February. Edwin D. Morgan of New York was selected as the first chairman and held the post until 1864. There have been forty-six chairmen since Morgan.

Where do the state and local party organizations fit into national party structures?

For practical purposes, even though the United States is said to have a two-party system, there are, in effect, one hundred separate parties in this country, two in each state, which operate under the big umbrellas of the national committees. These state committees are, in fact, independent units, separate from the national party organization. City and county organizations on down to the local level operate under the state party structure.

The chief functions of the state and local committees are to raise funds, conduct registration drives, and develop the best possible candidates to run on party tickets.

How are state and local party leaders selected?

The theoretical model, from which deviations do exist, portrays authority flowing from the bottom up rather than from the top down.

In other words, precinct party members pick their precinct leader. The precinct leaders, in turn, vote for the ward leader. The ward leaders decide who the county or city chairman will be. Those chairmen, in turn, determine who fills the state leader's post and so on up to the national level.

What discipline do the parties' national committees exercise over state and local committees and officials?

Very little, really. Although state and local party leaders and their organizations are expected to support their party's national ticket, some have been known to either bolt and support opposing party candidates or even "sit out" elections. The only discipline the national party has over such situations is the threat of expulsion, which is seldom employed and not always effective. Most state and local party leaders consider themselves outside of the national committee jurisdiction anyway.

What does a voter owe his party? In turn, what discipline does a party hold over its members?

A voter who commits himself to one party or the other owes that party its support as long as its views, programs, and policies are in line with his own. But a political party cannot enforce the loyalty of its members, let alone exercise discipline over elected officials from its own ranks.

Just what are the functions of the Democratic and Republican national committees?

The most important function of each national committee is to schedule, plan, and conduct its party's presidential nominating convention every four years. In addition, the committees help to direct the presidential campaigns and maintain national headquarters in Washington, which raise funds to finance party work and to provide continuity of party activities between elections. Included in these activities are research, public relations, and voter identification and registration programs.

Who makes up the membership of the national committees?

The membership of the Republican National Committee is made up of one state chairman from each of the fifty states and a committeeman and committeewoman from each of the fifty states and the District of Columbia, Puerto Rico, the Virgin Islands, and Guam—a total of 158 members. As a result of party reorganizations made by the Democrats at their 1972 national convention, the Democratic National Committee is now composed of 303 members, including 150 whose seats are apportioned among the states on the basis of population and support of the party's presidential candidates.

How are national committeemen and committeewomen chosen?

Although nominated by their respective states, national committeemen and committeewomen are officially elected or confirmed by the national convention every four years.

How are national party chairmen selected?

Technically, by a vote of members of the national committee.

Practically, however, when one of the parties nominates a new candidate for president or already has a president in the White House, the committee members usually acquiesce in his recommendation for chairman. When the party is out of power, key leaders often agree in advance on the person to be selected, and the national committee ratifies their choice.

Are the chairmen of the two national parties paid?

Neither Mrs. Jean Westwood, named Democratic National Chairman in 1972, nor Sen. Robert Dole, picked for the job as GOP National Chairman in 1971, were paid salaries. Both were reimbursed for expenses incurred in connection with their jobs, however. In the past, some party chairmen have been paid salaries and some have not, depending upon their outside activities, income, and whether they worked full or part time at the job.

How about Democratic and Republican state chairmen? Are they paid?

In most cases, they are not. Approximately one-half of the Democratic state chairmen are paid salaries and about one-third of the GOP chairmen. In states where chairmen are not paid salaries, they are usually compensated for expenses. Most state party organizations have executive directors who are salaried, however.

How big are the Democratic and Republican national committee staffs?

The Republican National Committee staff operates with under two hundred employees in nonelection years and the Democratic Committee with less than one hundred. Both staffs usually double or triple in size during presidential campaigns.

Where do political organizations get their money? For instance, how do local Democratic and Republican clubs pay their bills?

Local clubs utilize fund-raising drives, either by direct mail or personal appeal or by special events such as dinners. They have no sources but themselves. In fact, they very often are assessed by state party organizations to help finance their activities and overhead. In a few cases, an older club, city, or county organization may have accumulated revenue-producing assets, such as rental property donated or willed to it by a staunch supporter. But virtually all conduct fund-raising programs to maximize the resources available to assist local candidates' campaigns.

How about the national committees of the two parties? How do they raise funds?

Roughly the same way—through direct mail solicitation, with each party mailing literally millions of letters annually to potential contributors, and through party affairs, such as fund-raising dinners. But the biggest single way of reaching contributors and raising money is direct mail.

In addition to the Republican and Democratic national committees, which other party committees operate at the national level?

There are three major ones in each party, all headquartered in the nation's capital. On the GOP side, they are:

1. The Republican Congressional Committee. One of the oldest of the political committees (sometimes called the Republican Congressional Campaign Committee), this one was established in 1866 by GOP members of the House of Representatives who felt they needed an organization separate from the party's national committee to help in their election campaigns. In business ever since, the committee's membership is made up of one House member from each state in which the party has representation in the U.S. House. The staff consists of forty full-time employees, most of whom are professionals in campaign work, who provide a wide range of services, assistance, and funds to both GOP House incumbents and challengers for Democratic-held seats. The chairman in 1972 was Rep. Bob Wilson of California, who had held the post since 1961.

2. The Republican Senatorial Campaign Committee. Although the GOP Congressional Committee had at first provided campaign assistance and funds to both Senate and House members, adoption of the Seven-

teenth Amendment to the Constitution in 1913 was the deciding factor in the establishment of a committee to assist GOP senators exclusively in their campaigns. Thus, the Republican Senatorial Campaign Committee was formally organized in 1919. The new committee did not become a major force in Senate campaigns, however, until after the 1948 elections when its staff was beefed up and it embarked on extensive fund-raising programs to help finance the campaigns of GOP senators and challengers. The staff consists of half-a-dozen members. The chairman in 1972 was Sen. Peter H. Dominick of Colorado, who was elected to the post in 1971. Unlike the House committee, the chairman cannot serve in a year in which he is up for reelection.

3. The Republican Governors Association (RGA). Organized in 1963, this committee was set up to help reelect GOP governors and to elect party challengers to governors' posts held by Democrats. It provides campaign know-how and funds to its candidates. All of the Republican governors, including the governors of four territories, are members of the RGA, and its chairmanship rotates every year. The staff is small in size—only three members. The 1972 chairman was Gov. William G. Milliken of Michigan.

On the Democratic side, these three committees operate nationally:

1. The Democratic Congressional Committee. Founded in 1882, this committee was set up with the same objective as its counterpart, the Republican Congressional Committee, only in this case to help elect Democrats to the U.S. House of Representatives. It employs a permanent staff of above 10 and maintains offices on Capitol Hill. The Committee's membership consists of one Congressman from each state having party representation in the House. It raises and disburses funds, prepares voting records on the opposition, supplies campaign literature, and acts in an advisory capacity for Democratic incumbents and challengers. In 1972, the chairman was Rep. Thomas P. O'Neill, Jr., of Massachusetts.

2. The Democratic Senatorial Campaign Committee. Established in 1916, this committee, like its Republican counterpart, was created to provide campaign assistance, primarily funds, to members of its party seeking reelection to the Senate or to Democratic challengers for Republican Senate seats. The chairman in 1972 was Sen. Ernest F. Hollings of South Carolina, and the committee's staff consists of about half a dozen members. Its chairmanship rotates every two years.

3. The Democratic Governors Caucus. This committee was set up in the early 1960s to raise funds and provide campaign assistance to Democratic governors seeking reelection and to party challengers seeking to un-

seat GOP governors. Every Democratic governor is a member of the association, and its 1972 chairman was Gov. Marvin Mandel of Maryland.

How about groups which operate on the fringes of the major parties, like the Americans for Democratic Action (ADA) on the Democratic side and the American Conservative Union (ACU) and the Ripon Society on the Republican side? How much influence do they have on party positions?

Not as much as the coverage they receive in the news media would suggest. In fact, the memberships of such groups are usually relatively small—approximately fifty thousand dues-paying members in the ADA, some fifty thousand in the ACU, and less than one thousand in the Ripon Society.

Like most groups which seek to move the major parties in one direction or the other—and there are many besides those just cited, of course—they are viewed with some skepticism by the party professionals, who often regard their public pronouncements as more divisive than reformative. Nevertheless, these organizations represent a point of view which contributes to the decision-making process, even though no one of them alone carries enough weight to actually sway public positions their way.

I'm still confused. Did the third-party candidacy of George C. Wallace help or hurt Richard Nixon in 1968?

It hurt. According to a postelection study by the Survey Research Center of the University of Michigan, Wallace's candidacy attracted a lot of Democrats who would probably have kicked over their party traces and voted for Nixon had Wallace not been in the race. The Michigan study showed that 45 percent of the people who voted for Wallace considered themselves Democrats, 41 percent independents, and 14 percent Republicans. On the so-called "warmth-coolness" scale, which measured voters feelings about the three candidates, half of the Wallace voters felt "cold" toward Humphrey, but only 26 percent felt that way about Nixon. In short, Nixon was more palatable to the Wallace voters than Humphrey and presumably would have received the bulk of their votes if the Alabamian had not been in the race.

What's the largest vote a minor-party candidate for president received?

Governor George Wallace's 1968 total of 9,906,473 (13.5 percent of the total cast) votes was the biggest. The next was Robert M. LaFollette who garnered 4,832,532 votes (16.6 percent) in 1924 as a Progressive party candidate. Running on the Bull Moose ticket in 1912, former President Theodore Roosevelt received 4,216,020 votes (27.5 percent). Governor Strom Thurmond of South Carolina polled 1,176,125 votes (2.4 percent) as a States' Rights candidate in 1948. Former Vice President Henry A. Wallace, in that same election, drew 1,157,326 votes (2.4 percent) as the candidate of the Progressive party.

What is the breakdown on party strength?

According to a 1972 Gallup poll, 25 percent of the more than 140 million potential voters age eighteen and above viewed themselves as Republicans, 44 percent as Democrats, and 31 percent as independents. If voters were required to register with one major party or the other, abandoning their independent status, Gallup reports they would break down this way: 29 percent Republican, 50 percent Democratic, and 21 percent undecided.

How do you account for the decline in recent years in the number of voters who identify themselves with one party or the other?

An oversimplified answer is indifference—on the part of such key persons as presidents who sometimes consider themselves above politics and abandon their role as party leader, on the part of party officials who have other responsibilities and interests, and on the part of voters to whom party labels have come to mean less and less. In fact, the Gallup poll reported that 84 percent of the voters feel that, generally speaking, it is better to vote for the man over the party. Only 12 percent said they would vote for the party and four percent had no opinion.

Despite this finding by Gallup, most voters still tend to stick to party labels in supporting candidates for office. As Richard Scammon and Ben Wattenberg noted about past elections in *The Real Majority:*

> Eisenhower was most popular as "the man" in 1956, when he received 58 percent of the total vote. But 85 percent of Democrats still voted for Adlai Stevenson. In 1964, Barry Goldwater was alienating Americans by tens of millions, yet 80 percent of Republicans still voted for him. Franklin Roosevelt was an extremely popular "man," yet even in his peak year of 1936, the great majority of Republicans voted for Alf Landon. Perhaps the best that can be said of the apparent discrepancies in the man versus party data is that partisan Americans tend to think it is *their party* that usually nominates the best *man.*

In short, because it is popular these days to be an independent thinker, most voters tend to *think* they vote for the best man regardless of party, and therefore respond accordingly to questions about their voting habits. At the same time, they respond to questions about their party affiliation in a similar vein—stressing their independence rather than their partisanship.

If the country is as heavily Democratic as the statistics suggest, why have Republican presidential candidates won three out of the five presidential elections from 1952 to 1968?

For one thing, the data on the number of Democratic, Republican and independent voters isn't always reflective of how they cast their ballots on election day. Particularly attractive candidates draw voters across party lines and independents into their ranks, as Dwight D. Eisenhower did in 1952 and 1956.

Comment authors Scammon and Wattenberg, "If one added up all the Democratic and Republican votes for President since World War II, they would be about dead even: 185 million for Republicans and 186 million for Democrats. Some Democratic era!"

How about governorships? Which party dominates?

The Democratic party had the majority of the governors in 1972 with thirty versus twenty for the Republicans. However, nineteen of the state chief executives were up for reelection in 1972, including eleven Democrats and eight Republicans.

The Republicans obtained the majority of the governorships in 1967 with a 26–24 edge. In 1968, they gained four more and in 1969 two more, making the total thirty-two Republicans versus eighteen Democrats. But in 1970, the Democrats made the most remarkable comeback of any party since 1938 when they won thirteen gubernatorial seats from the Republicans while losing only two of their own, for a new balance of twenty-nine Democrats versus twenty-one Republicans. In 1971, the Democrats retrieved the Kentucky governorship, increasing their margin to 30 to 20.

How about the U.S. Congress? Of the 100 members of the Senate, how many are Democrats and how many Republicans?

The Democrats had a 1972 majority in the Senate of 55 to 45. Included in those figures were Sen. James Buckley who won election as a New York Conservative party candidate, and Sen. Harry Byrd, Jr., of Virginia, who ran as an independent. Buckley caucused with the Republicans and Byrd with the Democrats. Of the one-third of the Senate members up for reelection in 1972, 19 seats were held by Republicans and 14 by Democrats.

What is the House breakdown?

There were 254 Democrats in the House in 1972 and 177 Republicans, plus four vacancies at election time. All 435 House seats are up for election every two years, of course.

Which party controls the most legislatures?

On the eve of the 1972 elections, the Democrats held the majority. They had complete control of both houses in sixteen states while the Republicans dominated only nine.

In terms of separate bodies, the Democrats also held the majority, controlling twenty-nine upper houses versus eighteen for the Republicans, with one tied. In the lower houses, the Democrats were dominant in twenty-eight, the Republicans in twenty. Actually, Nebraska has only one house and is the only unicameral legislature in the country which also is nonpartisan. The other nonpartisan state with two houses is Minnesota.

I'm not entirely convinced. Are political parties really necessary?

Yes, for these reasons:

1. They provide the glue that keeps the country's political structure intact between elections.

2. They enable voters who haven't studied the issues or the candidates (and this is a majority in each election) to vote on the basis of the party's philosophy and achievement as well as its program for the future.

3. They enable voters to hold accountable the party in power, instead of scattered individuals, for unresolved problems and unfulfilled promises, and to "throw the rascals out" and vote in the other party next time.

4. They provide the foundation for a continuing "loyal opposition" which enables the party out of power to serve as a watchdog over the activities of the party in office.

5. They provide incentives for close cooperation among elected officials of the same party to get the job done, a cooperation which would be largely nonexistent if party loyalty or indebtedness weren't present.

6. They stimulate a healthy competition, with each party seeking to outdo the other in its promises and performances in meeting the needs of the electorate.

7. They help to surface the best candidates for public office, since each one must ordinarily run the gamut of party approval before standing before the voters for election, and they provide in most cases campaign assistance in the form of workers and funds to help elect them.

CHAPTER 3

Why get involved?

That's what I really want to know—why should I get involved in politics? What's in it for me?

The chief tangible return is the satisfaction of working for a goal that means something to you. If a candidate impresses you as the type of person who should be in office in place of the incumbent, volunteer your services. If he wins, you'll not only have the unique personal fulfillment which comes from involvement in a successful campaign, you'll also be able to take pride in his public achievements.

Depending upon the circumstances, you might even want to seek full-time employment in a political campaign or with one of the major parties. But there are usually far more volunteers than salaried staff members in political campaigns, particularly at the local level. And competition is usually intense for the comparatively few paid jobs.

A somewhat overworked cliché also explains why people should get active in campaigns. Corny as it may sound, it has a lot of truth to it. "Political action" is the phrase. When properly organized and staffed with highly motivated people, it produces results, including changes in the status quo.

Mayor John Lindsay's first campaign for mayor of New York City in 1965 was an excellent demonstration of how to beat the so-called machine. The Democratic organization had the vast majority of the registered voters in the city. But Lindsay, running at the time as a Republican, won the election through the broad-based support of a large number of volunteers and a well-run campaign. This showed that a minority party or group could field a candidate who could win.

Even the presidency is not invulnerable to political action. Former Democratic Congressman Allard Lowenstein of New York is credited with starting the "Dump Johnson" movement which contributed to President Lyndon B. Johnson's decision not to seek reelection in 1968. Lindsay's and Lowenstein's efforts are examples of effective political action.

In sum, getting involved in politics can be almost anything you want it to be and for more than one motivation. Ideally, the involvement will stem from conviction to effect an improvement in government, be it a change in policy or the election of a candidate.

As Sen. Margaret Chase Smith of Maine once noted, "If you make just a little dent along the way, you've made an important contribution."

You still haven't convinced me. How important is it for me to get involved in politics?

Very. Frederick Pohl, writing in his book, *Practical Politics 1972*, puts it this way: "How much time is your government worth to you? It costs you a fair chunk of your income. It may cost you your life—it can draft you and send you off to die in a war; it can fail to protect you against murderers and traffic speeders; it can destroy your job and let you starve."

How important is all this to you?

What about my convictions? Will I have to sacrifice them if I get involved in politics?

If your principles are narrow and rigid, the answer is yes. Former Congressman T. V. Smith of Illinois, once observed, "A man is not a good man who will compromise the core of himself—that is, the final principles by which he lives. But a man is not a good citizen who does not meet other citizens half way."

If I decided to make a career out of politics, how much could I expect to earn annually? How does this compare with business or the professions?

The range is from a very nominal salary up to six figures, the latter being the president of the United States, whose salary is $200,000 a year. Basically, there are four categories of career political employment.

First is elected office. The president, as noted, earns the highest amount of any elected official. Members of Congress are paid $42,500 annually; governors' salaries range from $10,000 in Arkansas up to $85,000 in New York; members of the state legislatures earn anywhere from simple travel and expense allowances while in session up to $19,200 a year in California; salaries for mayors, county and township officials, and similar elected posts vary widely, depending chiefly upon the population of the political unit.

The second category covers the federal and state appointive positions, such as cabinet officers, heads of agencies and commissions, and the like on down to the state and local level. Federal cabinet salaries now are $60,000 a year; state cabinet posts range well up above $40,000 in such states as New York.

Third is the appointive staff group. Included are assistants to such officials as the president, cabinet officers, governors, members of Congress, state legislators, and mayors. The ceiling now is over $40,000 in the case of presidential assistants and in excess of $30,000 for congressional assistants and top committee staff personnel. In the bigger states, salaries for posts of comparable responsibility are in the $20,000 range.

The fourth category consists of paid staff members at the national, state, and local levels of the major parties—committee chairmen, executive directors, campaign organizers, public relations directors, etc.—whose annual earnings range from $35,000 on down to simple reimbursement for expenses.

Although salaries in federal elective and appointive posts are on a par or even slightly higher than in comparable positions in private industry, salaries for professional staff members of the various party committees are slightly under levels in nonpolitical activity.

Okay, let's say I've decided I want to get involved. Where and how do I start?

Assuming you've already decided on your party affiliation, there are four basic ways of getting involved, all tied into joining an existing political organization or one which is in the process of formation: (1) a local political club; (2) a political party organization in your area; (3) a campaign in behalf of an individual candidate; or (4) a campaign for or against a specific issue.

Probably the easiest place to start is the precinct in which you reside. As the lowest unit of political organization, the precinct—or district or division as it is called in some states—usually constitutes anywhere from a few square blocks in an urban area to several square miles in rural areas. Altogether, there are 164,000 precincts in this country, averaging 850 voters

each (of which about 500 actually go to the polls). Many of these are in
need of captains or workers to contact voters at election time, to serve as
poll watchers, election judges, and many other jobs in the area on behalf
of party candidates. Contact the local party leader in your area to get
started.

What'll come of all this? Sen. Hugh Scott of Pennsylvania, Republican
Leader in the U.S. Senate, said it this way: "So you begin your apprentice-
ship in the great art of politics and, in time, you will either grow bored
with the whole thing, or it will get into your blood and you're a gone
gosling. You are likely to be politicking all your life."

What kind of activities could I become involved in?

There are many. Here are a few:

In public relations—working on publicity, including the development
of a coordinated program to obtain the best possible exposure in the newspapers and over radio and television; preparing news releases; researching
opposing candidates or major issues in the campaign; designing brochures
and campaign material, assisting in their distribution, and planning and
putting out mailings.

In programming—planning programs to promote your candidates or
cause, including receptions and fund-raising dinners; setting up a "Speakers' bureau" and arranging engagements for speakers; planning and running rallies, organizing parades, and even manning sound trucks and
setting up caravans to visit shopping centers; handling the bookkeeping
for these events, including receipts and expenditures; and working on the
scheduling of candidates for maximum impact.

In precinct work—preparing voter index cards and lists; making phone
calls to get people to register and vote; house-to-house canvassing; recruiting party workers; providing transportation to polls on election day; serving
as an elections clerk or a poll watcher; working as a block or precinct captain, or even as a ward or county leader.

The key to success in politics is to demonstrate willingness, imagina-
tion, and industry. Get to know as many of the key people in the party or
campaign organization as you can. Impress them with your energy and
ability. Before long, you'll be tapped for positions of greater responsibility,
perhaps even to run for office yourself. One caution: be frank in analyzing
your own strengths and weaknesses. If you don't like research work, for
example, stay away from it in the campaign even if a position opens. To
accept an important responsibility knowing you can't effectively handle
it obviously will do you more harm than good. And it won't help the
campaign either.

Teddy Roosevelt had this sage advice for fledgling politicians: "Do what you can, with what you have, where you are."

What if my time is limited? I really have no desire to go around ringing doorbells in my neighborhood or anything like that. Is there much point in my volunteering?

As someone once said, "You'll never know if you don't try."

A friend of ours in New York City had the same problem in 1968. An executive with one of the largest companies in the country, he had only a limited amount of time. But he was enthusiastic about New York Governor Nelson Rockefeller making the run for the Republican presidential nomination.

Since he was a very organized, methodical, intelligent individual, something involving analysis but not requiring him to be at a specific place at a definite time seemed to be the answer. Accordingly, he contacted one of Rockefeller's key assistants and spelled it out.

The result was that he and a number of other bright young executives were formed into an issue-study group. They received assignments which they did on their own time and turned in when completed. These involved such undertakings as researching issues, including pro and con views, and compiling data on positions taken by other candidates for the nomination.

The young man in question felt tremendously challenged by the work. He was able to do it in his office, at home, and even travelling on the subway. He ultimately became quite expert in one field, agriculture, a subject about which he previously knew virtually nothing.

The campaign manager and his assistants know what their needs are. For example, they might have an activity scheduled where they are worried about the size of the crowd which may turn out for the candidate. Your assignment: work up a plan to pack the event to overflowing.

Or maybe you could make fifty phone calls the week preceding election to a list that headquarters will provide you along with a suggested script. The list of possible one-shot kinds of activities that can be planned for a campaign can be quite long.

Depending on your qualifications, attitude, and performance, you can expect to find your way into a meaningful campaign position. It may sound a bit rosy, but anyone who really wants to work can find plenty of opportunities in a well-organized campaign.

Campaign organizations, however, are not always models of carefully structured business operations like, for example, big corporations. They frequently are rushed, haphazard, and disorganized. One reason is that they are usually put together on a crash basis, oftentimes relying extensively on volunteers whose time availability may be limited. So be prepared to find a lot of enthusiasm and less administrative sophistication.

Don't rule yourself out, in other words. Make the overture to the campaign organization leaders and let them tell you whether they can use you and how.

How are volunteers recruited to work in a campaign? I've never been asked.

You're not alone. The problem with many campaign organizations is the lack of an effective program to attract, train, and utilize volunteers. There are several techniques that are employed, however, all of which boil down to either direct contact—that is, by mail, telephone, or person-to-person—or advertising.

Direct contact, which is usually the most effective, involves various approaches, starting with friends of the candidate. He should list every potential supporter he can. Then they should be called or sent a personal letter asking them to either participate in the campaign or contribute funds to the campaign. Supporters thus recruited should be asked, in turn, to recruit their friends, and so on.

Another way to recruit volunteers is through registered voter lists, if they are available and if they indicate party affiliation, as well as through party worker lists. A letter can be effective or even better a visit.

Another method that is less frequently employed but which can yield dividends is to make a canvass of voters. From the results, the names of those who indicate they favor the candidate are selected, and they are either called or sent personal letters asking them to volunteer.

Paid advertisements in newspapers or other publications can include a clip-out coupon enabling potential volunteers to indicate the type of campaign activity in which they are interested. Such ads provide double mileage in that they advertise the candidate as well as induce individuals to become active participants in the campaign. A similar technique can be used in radio or TV advertising, with a phone number or address listed to contact for further information or to sign up.

What kind of experience should volunteers have?

Experience is not required to join a campaign. If you have certain skills, all the better. A well-planned campaign will have a great number of potential projects whose implementation is heavily dependent on one thing: people. That's where you come in.

At the same time, you might discover unused talents. One congressional candidate defeated an incumbent several years ago in a campaign in which he had volunteers doing things they never tried before. A quiet, unassuming young lawyer had a long-time yearning to be a cartoonist. But he had never tried his hand at it; sophisticated doodling was the extent of his artistic experience. The candidate's press assistant, who prepared a regular in-house newsletter for distribution to the volunteer corps and other supporters, encouraged the lawyer to try it. The results were remarkable and enhanced the quality of the publication substantially.

In short, the basic requirement for a volunteer is the willingness to help. If the campaign staff is on the ball, work will be found.

Is there such a thing as too many volunteers in a campaign?

If the campaign is properly run, no. But as a practical matter, overly busy campaign managers too often fail to come up with assignments for volunteers, causing them to lose interest.

Since an undesirable development in a campaign is for volunteers to feel unneeded or unwanted, the campaign manager should, if worst comes to worst, develop "make-work" projects to keep them busy. One recruiting effort in a recent campaign paid off so well that campaign projects were screened by the manager and his aides to determine which could be adapted to using up the manpower pool available. One result was that campaign mailing pieces which were normally folded automatically by the printer's machine were left unfolded so that thousands of pieces would pass through the hands of the volunteers. This type of make-work activity can be avoided, however, by adequate planning.

Can a campaign function without volunteers?

By best estimates, a well-organized campaign which has workers right down to the precinct level can boost the vote for party candidates by 5 percent or more. This bonus results from the personal contact and the enthusiasm that dedicated volunteers are able to convey on behalf of candidates to voters who might otherwise stay at home.

On that basis, volunteers must be considered an essential ingredient in any campaign. Political campaigns, if they have the financial resources, could function without volunteers. But most lack the funds to do so and therefore must rely on these human resources.

Is there any relationship between the level of education and affluence and whether people will volunteer to work in campaigns?

Surveys show that the level of political awareness and interest corresponds to a great extent to education and income levels.

Those at the bottom of the income spectrum or who did not complete high school show less interest in volunteering their serivces than do business executives, married women with college degrees, and professional people. But part of the lack of participation may be related to whether persons in lower educational and income levels have ever been asked to participate. They mistakenly may feel, as might be expected in cases of those unfamiliar with politics, that they need pull or influence to get involved in a campaign.

Are volunteers expected to contribute money to the campaign?

Not usually. Their contribution is their time. However, there is nothing which rules out donations by individuals who can afford it and wish to do so. As a rule, the percentage actually giving money probably would be low, and the amount of those contributions would be small as well.

Any campaign organization that attempts to dun its own volunteer force of ordinary people for funds is heading for trouble. Morale very likely would deteriorate, as might the size of the volunteer organization.

How do party professionals view volunteers?

As essential, but also with some skepticism.

Volunteers are the same as money. They represent labor that doesn't cost precious dollars and cents. Having them on board permits the implementation of efforts which otherwise would not be possible.

Ideally, for instance, a well-organized campaign will have at least one party worker in every precinct. A force like that enables the organization to make door-to-door contacts delivering campaign literature, making canvasses of registered voters, recruiting volunteers, and so on. Many such activities could not be undertaken without volunteers.

However, because these workers are not on the campaign payroll, and therefore not subject to the same staff discipline as paid workers, they are often viewed apprehensively by party professionals who are wary of their reliability. Some volunteers frequently work abbreviated schedules or fail to show up when needed, contributing to this attitude. But because no campaign can afford to maintain a payroll down to the precinct level, most party professionals welcome volunteers into their ranks, and keep their fingers crossed.

Another advantage also accrues from recruiting large numbers of volunteers, even if they do little or nothing. Membership makes them feel they are a part of the organization, and thus the chances of holding their votes and possibly those of their friends are excellent.

How are local party organizations structured?

An elected chairman or president is usually the chief officer. There's a board or executive committee which itself is elected, generally by the ward leaders. There is usually a vice-chairman, secretary, treasurer and other positions as in any organization. Each ward and precinct will be represented by a committeeman, again usually elected but sometimes appointed depending upon the locality. The structure is a pyramid with a chairman at the top.

Interestingly, the party organization with complete representation in every single precinct is the exception rather than the rule. If more than 50 percent of the precincts are organized, that's considered good.

That's why a candidate who anticipates a close race will tend not to rely solely on the local party structure. Instead, formidable as the task is, he may well set out to create his own organization. The party itself will provide certain assistance, of course. But the burden of the campaign will be carried by the candidate's own organization, exclusively oriented toward his needs. Once such an organization is established, whatever the regular party does is a bonus.

How can a local organization be built up, if there's none presently in existence?

A nucleus leadership group should be formed first. Its task is to lay out its objectives and develop a plan to achieve them, much as any business organization would function. The first orders of business are to publicize the new organization, recruit members for it, and raise funds.

Publicity for the group can usually be obtained by a simple news release announcing its formation, which is sent to newspapers (daily, weekly, and even shopping news), radio and TV stations, and any other publications which circulate in the area. The press release should be written in an easy-to-read news style, carrying the specifics about the group such as the names of its president or chairman and its key members, its objectives, and whom to contact for further information.

Recruiting can be accomplished in various ways, starting with a request to each member of the organizing group to list friends and acquaintances whom they think might be interested in joining up. These people should then be sent an invitation to the next meeting, followed up by a telephone call or personal contact. A newspaper ad appeal is another way of reaching potential members, if funds permit.

A reason to join the campaign obviously has to be offered. Think it through and develop a program along these lines. The recruiting effort should be continued through the life of the campaign. Minimally, it results in a commitment from an individual to vote for the candidate. Any work he performs and funds he contributes are bonuses.

Motivation is the key to maintaining the strength of any organization. It can be bolstered through a sense of participation, either real or imagined, performing a job or contributing money. Periodic meetings of supporters and candidates are helpful. Other means of communication, such as newsletters, also are employed in many campaigns to reinforce motivation.

An organizational framework into which the recruits are fitted is a necessity. In other words, develop specific requirements for which the manpower can be used. There usually will be a central headquarters with one or more outlying offices. People will be needed to man those facilities so that the public has access to materials and information and sees a continuing evidence of the campaign. Thus, a schedule for manning the facility should be drawn up and assignments of hours made. Frequently, those headquarters are also the locations at which the volunteers' work is done—stuffing envelopes, running off news releases, telephoning voters, etc.

Additionally, many campaigns either use the existing ward and precinct framework or a variation. A ward captain is appointed who then works to flesh out the organization, pyramiding downward with precinct captains and volunteers within the precincts. Once manned, that type of organization provides another basis for reaching the voters.

In addition to a force to canvass door to door, it offers the vehicle for scheduling neighborhood gatherings such as coffees, cocktail parties, receptions, and similar events where local residents can meet the candidate. Further, input to the main headquarters can come from these individuals about upcoming events. For example, if the local church is having a fish fry, the candidate might be able to arrange his schedule to drop in on the gathering. Other valuable information can be passed along as well, such as what the opposition may be doing in a particular area.

Although I consider myself an independent, if I went to work for the candidate of one of the major parties, would that make me a member of his party? Would I have to vote in the party primary?

The answer to both questions is no.

People who consider themselves independents, i.e., neither Republicans nor Democrats, frequently are found in the ranks of campaign workers for the candidate of one of the major parties. Their active participation is really an extension of their voting preference. It places no burden on them for party membership.

If your candidate is in a close primary race, however, you may want to consider registering in his party and voting for him on election day. He may need your vote as well as your campaign participation.

What's the difference between primary and general elections?

The primary is the party election which is held sometime between March and October to select the candidates who will run under the party's banner in the November general election. In short, the candidates whose names appear on the ballot in November are there in most cases because they won the right to be there in a party primary.

If you want to change your party and its candidates, the primary is the place to start. Sen. Hugh Scott of Pennsylvania sums up the reason for primary voting this way: "Don't you want something better than the lesser of two evils? That is the kind of selection you may find yourself making at the general election, when no interest has been shown at the primaries in the selection of party candidates."

If I vote in a party primary, do I have to vote for the same party candidates in November?

Of course not. There is no law, custom, or even moral obligation requiring you to do so. In fact, the secrecy of the ballot assures your complete freedom of choice.

In some states, however, if you vote in one party's primary, you may be barred from voting in the opposing party's primary next time. But again, this applies only to primaries and does not affect your choices in the general election.

Why should I bother to vote?

Why should you bother to bathe? Isn't making sure government is kept clean important, too? Besides, the importance of your single vote has been demonstrated over and over again by elections that were literally won and lost by that margin.

Can one vote really be that important in an election?

The wisdom of hindsight shows that a single vote, or a comparative handful, has been significant in numerous instances in American history.

A classic example occurred about one hundred years ago in the Hayes-Tilden presidential contest. Rutherford B. Hayes became the chief executive by virtue of a single electoral vote. But because his election was contested, it was referred to an electoral commission. Here again Hayes won by a single vote. The commission member casting the deciding vote was an Indiana congressman, an attorney who himself had been elected by only one vote. The deciding vote for the congressman was cast by a client who, though seriously ill, demanded to be taken to the polls so that he could cast his ballot. An unusual example, the story does illustrate that one person's vote indeed can be significant.

In 1960, approximately 69 million turned out for the presidential election which was won by then-Senator John F. Kennedy. The loser, outgoing Vice President Richard M. Nixon, would have come out on top if a mere 15,000 had voted for him instead of John F. Kennedy in four key states—Hawaii, Illinois, Missouri and South Carolina.

Is it possible to vote in the general election for some candidates of one party and some of another?

Of course. In fact, this is called ticket splitting, a device which has become rather widespread in recent years. In 1968, for example, voters in some 130 congressional districts, 32.4 percent of the total number of districts, cast their ballots for the presidential candidate of one party and for the congressional candidate of another. A half-century ago, ticket splitting of this kind was practically unknown. In the elections of 1920, only 3.2 percent of the congressional districts voted one party for president and another for Congress.

The 1970 elections provide another example of extensive ticket splitting. Of the twenty-three states in which there was both a gubernatorial and a senatorial contest, eleven, or nearly half, split their tickets and elected a governor from one party and a senator from another. The breakdown: six states elected a Republican senator and a Democratic governor, and four states elected a Democratic senator and a GOP governor. In New York, Republican Nelson Rockefeller was reelected governor, but Conservative party candidate James L. Buckley was elected senator over the Democratic and Republican candidates.

Actually, doesn't ticket splitting make sense—to elect a president of one party, for instance, and the Congress of another to keep an eye on the executive branch?

Although the watchdog theory is still prevalent in some quarters, it does tend to produce deadlocks between the two branches over the enactment of legislation and the administration of government. In *The Party's Over*, David S. Broder sums up his concern about the growing trend toward ticket splitting:

> It seems to me we would ask, before splitting a ticket, what it is we hope to accomplish by dividing between the parties the responsibility for government of our country, our state and our community. Do we think there is no difference between the parties? Do we distrust them both so thoroughly that we wish to set them against each other? Do we think one man so superior in virtue and wisdom that he must be put in office, no matter who accompanies him there? Why are we splitting our tickets? My guess is that, if we asked those questions, we would more often be inclined to give a temporary grant of power to one party at a time, rather than dividing responsibility so skillfully between the parties that neither can govern. If we were willing to risk this strategy, knowing that we would be able to throw the rascals out if they failed, we might even discover to our amazement that they are not always rascals.

What are the advantages and disadvantages of being an independent voter?

Although a sizable percentage of citizens claim to vote for the man rather than the party, as noted in Chapter 2, the fact of political life is that being an independent has more disadvantages than advantages. For one thing, it's limiting. If you are really interested in bettering government at all levels, it's important that you pick a party which most closely relates to your personal political philosophy and work within its structure to produce the best possible candidates for public office.

Since candidates for the general election in November are usually chosen by their respective parties in the primaries, the independent has no voice in the selection of who will be on the ballot. Unless he wants to write in the name or names of his own selections, he's stuck with a choice between the Democratic and Republican candidates.

Party affiliation, in short, gives him two cracks at selecting the best man for the job—in the primary where he can vote for the candidate of the party in which he registers and in the November general election. And keep in mind that since we use the secret ballot in this country, there is nothing to prevent the voter from voting for whichever party candidate he chooses in the general election.

There must be some advantages to being an independent.

The chief advantage is that it makes the job of exercising your responsibility as a citizen easier. You only have to vote once, in other words. In fact, as an independent, you aren't eligible to vote in either the Republican or Democratic primaries where party candidates are selected for the November general elections.

As Frederick Pohl put it in his book, *Practical Politics 1972*:

> Politicians love the independent voter. They will pat him on the head and compliment him on his steadfast resolution of purpose. They know that the man who values his independent judgement too much to submit to the dictates of a political party has put himself in the position where he can do nothing *but* submit to the dictates of a political party. When the basic decisions were made, he was home telling his wife what a principled man he was.

I heard it's against the law to donate your services to the government. Is this true?

Yes. A 1905 law prohibits the government from accepting voluntary service "except in cases of sudden emergency involving the loss of human life or destruction of property." This has generated what is called "dollar-a-year" men—business executives and others who respond to their country's call in time of crisis and accept a token payment of $1.00 annually for their services.

If I decided to run for office, what are some simple guidelines?

First and foremost, never forget that you are, in effect, applying for a job—the job of representing your particular constituency. In a sense, you are applying to the electorate, who will either say to you on election day, "Okay, the job is yours," or turn thumbs down on your application.

Keep in mind that a person applying for a job naturally shows himself off to the best advantage. He prepares himself carefully for the important interview with his prospective boss. He puts on his best suit of clothes. He smiles, even if a bit nervously. He has his qualifications at his fingertips. He is aware of the needs of the job and the problems of his boss, and has solutions to these problems in mind, if asked.

Before the candidate for public office gets the job he is seeking, he must convince his boss, the voters, that he is fitted for it, that he has the ability and temperament required, that he is a trustworthy and reliable human being, that he understands his constituents' needs and is prepared to fight for them.

In short, the voters have got to like the candidate. They must find his personality friendly and inspiring. They should feel that in him they not only have an informed and competent representative, but a concerned and dedicated advocate. A sloppily dressed, morose, and impatient candidate isn't likely to elicit a positive response from the voters. But a warm and confident candidate is.

Aside from these general guidelines, the candidate should make a realistic assessment of his chances of winning before he gets in the race—the pluses and minuses of his personality, his background and experience, his standing in the community, his name recognition among voters, and how much money he can put into the campaign himself as well as raise from friends and supporters.

Is it necessary to start at the bottom and work my way up to a major office?

Not if your name happens to be Kennedy, Rockefeller, Reagan, Eisenhower, or something equally well-known. If you have the name-recognition and prestige of an Eisenhower or a Reagan or the money of a Kennedy or Rockefeller, there is no real reason to start anywhere but at the top.

However, since you probably have neither, your best course is to work within the party structure and with local party leaders, advancing up the ladder through the various elected offices that open up for you.

What do party leaders look for in a candidate for public office?

Before putting their blessing on him, party leaders want to know first and foremost: can he win? The potential candidate for office is closely scrutinized to determine whether he'll be a good campaigner and vote getter, how he'll project on television and before audiences, where he stands on issues, whether he'll be accepted by labor and/or business, and so forth. The personal life of the candidate is also probed. Is he happily married, or at least seemingly so? Will his wife be an asset or a liability to him? Is there anything in his private life that would mar his election chances if it surfaced?

Before Warren G. Harding was nominated at the 1920 Chicago GOP convention, Republican party leaders met in the now-famous "smoke-filled room" at the Blackstone Hotel, called Harding in, and asked him bluntly, "Is there anything in your private life that could affect your personal integrity or harm your chances of winning if it came out? If there is, we want to know it now."

Fortunately for Harding, whatever personal peccadilloes he had went undetected until years after his death.

Where does the word "candidate" come from?

The Romans originated it with *candidatus,* meaning clothed in white. The white togas the ancient Roman office seekers wore were intended to convey the idea of purity.

The word has the same root as candor, incandescent, and candle. Although Shakespeare used it in its Latin form, the term evolved into "candidateship" and then "candidature" in England. American usage initially was "candidature" but subsequently became "candidacy."

What does the phrase "You can't beat somebody with nobody" mean?

It summarizes the problem of a political unknown taking on a popular and well-known opponent. In wide use during the early 1900s, the phrase has been attributed to House Speaker Joseph G. Cannon, although it had antecedents in various forms as far back as Lincoln's presidency.

As used today, it concedes the formidable nature of opposing a highly regarded, apparently effective incumbent or a nonincumbent candidate with a strong reputation and high name identification. It's an uphill fight for an unknown in either instance.

Theodore Roosevelt popularized the term "hat in the ring" when he announced on February 21, 1912, that he planned to contest Republican President William Howard Taft for the GOP nomination that year. "My hat's in the ring," Roosevelt told a reporter. Roosevelt also had this sage advice for fledgling politicians: "Do what you can, with what you have, where you are." *From the Collections of the Library of Congress.*

What about the phrase "hat in the ring"? Where did it originate?

Originating in the western United States, the phrase was used in the last century to signal the willingness of a man to enter a boxing or wrestling contest. He would toss his hat into the ring—in other words, accept the challenge.

The term was popularized by former President Theodore Roosevelt in 1912 when he announced his intention to contest William Howard Taft for the Republican presidential nomination that year. While passing through Cleveland on February 21 to keep a speaking date in Columbus, Roosevelt was stopped by a reporter and asked whether he intended to run for the presidency. Replied Roosevelt, "My hat's in the ring."

Today, the phrase hat in the ring is still used in the way Roosevelt first meant it, as an announcement of active candidacy. It is also the name of a popular nonpartisan parlor game in which up to eight players contest each other for their party's presidential nomination.

PART 2

Politics: Campaigning for Office

CHAPTER 4

What's the voter like?

What percent of voters usually turn out for elections?

Far too few. In a presidential election, slightly over 60 percent of the citizens eligible to vote actually do so. Only about 45 percent turn out for off-year congressional elections to select the men and women who write the nation's laws. The turnout in state and local elections usually falls within this range.

Altogether, some fifty million voters can be counted on to sit out a presidential election. In fact, if all the people eligible who failed to vote in 1968 had banded together, supporting their own candidate for president, they could have elected him over Richard Nixon with fifteen million votes to spare.

I thought voter participation was on the increase.

Not so. Although the total number of voters has gone up, mainly because the population keeps rising, the actual percentage of those who take the time to go to the polls is on the decline. For instance, 62 percent of those eligible actually voted in the 1960 presidential election, 61.2 percent in 1964, and only 60.8 percent in 1968, a decline of 1.2 percent in eight years.

What's behind this nationwide decline? Although people may not be entirely aware of their reasons for not voting, suggests Dr. Pierre Purves, director of statistics for the National Republican Congressional Committee, "Underneath this [decline] is the feeling voting does not get you anywhere . . . with our high standards of living and general affluence, people feel secure and also feel it is unnecessary to vote."

Isn't there more to it than that?

Yes. The lack of motivation is a key element in nonvoting. Unless the voter is concerned about an issue which affects him directly or is influenced by a candidate he knows or particularly wants to support or see defeated, he is as likely as not to stay at home on election day.

If he decides to vote, however, he has another problem. Inside the voting booth, he'll find a ballot containing the titles of a dozen or more offices and the names of several dozen candidates seeking those offices, ranging from the president of the United States to a U.S. senator and a congressman, a state senator and an assemblyman, a county sheriff, local judge, the county tax assessor, and many others. Some of the offices he has never heard of, not to mention most of the candidates.

He may also be asked to decide several referendum questions on such knotty problems as a bond issue for a new school house or salary increases for the city's councilmen. Most of these issues are at best only vaguely familiar and at worst confusing in the highly legalistic language in which they are phrased.

So rather than vote for someone or something he may really be opposed to, he checks the candidates whose names are familiar, skips the rest, and ducks the public questions, unless one happens to call for busing his children or raising his property taxes. But the entire process is somewhat unnerving. No wonder he doesn't rush to the polls on election day.

Is there much difference between voter turnout in presidential versus off years? If so, why?

There usually is an appreciable dropoff in voter turnout in nonpresidential years. As an example, the 1970 voter turnout was somewhat under 57 million voters compared with the 73.2 million who cast ballots in the 1968 presidential year. Similarly, the 1966 off year brought out 57 million voters, again a marked decline from the 1964 total of 70 million.

Clearly, the presence of the presidential candidates on the ballot has a massive effect in stimulating voter turnout. Certain states, cities, or individual localities can buck the trend in the off years when a significant race takes place. But the nonpresidential years tend to exhibit declines in overall voter turnouts nationally, thus warranting the term "off" year.

What are the requirements for voting in national, state, and local elections?

Basically, you must be a citizen of the United States, eighteen years of age or older, and a resident of your state for at least thirty days. Prior to a 1972 Supreme Court decision, which struck down longer-than-30-day state residency requirements, the length of time varied from immediate eligibility in one state, Massachusetts, to three months in five states, six months in nineteen states, and one year in twenty-five states.

What's the difference between a plurality and a majority?

These two terms are often confused. However, there is a difference. When a candidate receives a majority, it means he has won more than half of the votes cast. When he receives a plurality—a term usually used when more than two candidates are in the race—it refers to the number of excess votes he has won over those of his closest opponent. The terms are sometimes used interchangeably when there are only two candidates in the race.

What's the average voter like? What's his age? Educational level?

If there is such a thing as an average voter, he or she looks something like this, according to U.S. Census Bureau data: middle aged, about forty-five years old; middle class, with an annual family income of just over $9,000; and with a high school diploma but no college degree.

In his book, *The Selling of a Candidate*, publicist Hal Evry describes the average voter:

> The average American voter is 45 years old. She is a caucasian female who likes red as a color and lilac as a scent. Her major interests are self-preservation, love and financial security.
>
> In terms of belonging, she is an American first, a Nebraskan (or Kentuckian, etc.) second and a member of an ethnic or self-interest group third. Then, deep down on the list of belonging, she is either a Democrat, Republican or Independent. Party affiliation is one of the least important matters in her life.
>
> She is married to a breadwinner who earns approximately $9,100 a year, and has two grown children who influence in a major way how she thinks about wars, crime, inflation and other matters of universal concern.
>
> She *thinks* she is slightly more conservative than liberal and, when pressed, she thinks that politics is slightly dishonest and she resents

mudslinging during a campaign. But her chief attitude toward politics and politicians is utter *apathy*. Together with most voters, she just doesn't give a darn about politics.

Except for the few weeks before an election, she can't tell you the name of her state representative or state senator or her Congressman. She doesn't know the latest voting record of anyone in public office. She has never contributed to a political campaign and has never attended a political meeting.

She can be reached through her emotions and is chiefly concerned with her physical and financial security. Any other appeal leaves her cold and unattuned.

When does the voter make up his mind who he's going to vote for?

In the case of presidential elections, surveys show that approximately one-third of the voters have made up their minds in advance of the nominating conventions, roughly one-third at the time of the conventions, and the remainder during varying times up to election day. In fact, a small percentage of the voters, perhaps up to 2 or 3 percent, don't make up their minds until they walk into the voting booth. The ratio of voters who have made up their minds before the nominating convention goes up to more than half if an incumbent president is seeking reelection.

Similar ratios apply to lesser offices as well, to varying degrees. Close to one-third of the voters will tend to cast ballots for their party's candidates, meaning they have made up their minds in advance of the nominations. Another one-third will decide after the nominations are made, and the remainder sometime prior to the election.

What percentage of the total population in this country is eligible to vote?

Approximately two-thirds.

How many eligible voters are there?

In the 1972 elections, 140 million, including some twenty-five million first-time voters eighteen through twenty-four years of age.

How does this compare with the 1968 election?

Up 19.4 million since 1968, due largely to the infusion of twenty-five million first-time voters—eleven million eighteen-to-twenty-year-olds and about fourteen million aged twenty-one to twenty-four who reached their majority since the 1968 election.

Of these new voters, how many are in college?

Approximately four million. Another 4.1 million hold full time jobs. About one million are housewives.

How many are in high school? The armed forces?

Nearly 900,000 are still in high school, and about 800,000 are in the armed forces.

Prior to the constitutional amendment granting the vote to eighteen-year-olds, didn't several states permit persons under twenty-one to vote?

Yes. Georgia and Kentucky permitted persons eighteen and older to vote, Alaska nineteen and above, and Hawaii twenty and above.

What was the average turnout by the under-twenty-one voters in those four states?

Poor. In the 1968 election, for instance, roughly one-third of the under-twenty-one eligibles actually voted. This compares with a better than 60 percent turnout for the twenty-one and above voters.

Which party will benefit most in the long run from the eighteen-to-twenty-year-old vote?

That's hard to tell. Prior to the 1972 elections, preliminary soundings indicated the Democratic party would be the biggest beneficiary. But, while the Democrats were listed as party preference by 35 percent of young people surveyed and the Republicans by 14 percent, the bulk, 51 percent, identified themselves as either independents or uncommitted. Thus, both parties have a great incentive to work to win over these emerging voters.

What's the political philosophy of these new voters?

According to a Gallup Poll released in May, 1972, the biggest segment of these voters, like their elders, consider themselves middle-of-the-roaders. Here is the breakdown: 38 percent middle-of-the-road; 35 percent fairly liberal; 8 percent very liberal; 8 percent fairly conservative; 5 percent very conservative. Six percent were unsure.

Just curious—does the political philosophy of people tend to change much as they grow older?

Yes, it usually becomes more conservative. Although the eighteen-to-twenty-year-olds cited in the preceding answer tend to be more liberal than conservative, their elders tend to be more conservative. Dr. Gallup chronicles this change in the following breakdown:

Age	Very conservative	Fairly conservative	Middle-of-the-road	Fairly liberal	Very liberal	No opinion
21–29	9	18	33	26	11	3
30–49	14	26	32	17	7	4
50 and over	20	24	31	13	7	5

Why was twenty-one first picked as the age to start voting?

Under English common law, men and women were considered to have reached maturity—"of age," in other words—at twenty-one. The American colonies adopted the same standard and applied it to the voting age after the Revolutionary War.

Which state has the most voters? Which the fewest?

As would be expected of the biggest state, California has the most voters—13.0 million, compared with 12.8 million in New York, and 8.2 million in Pennsylvania. Alaska has the smallest voting-age population with 200,000.

How about overseas personnel, such as members of the armed forces and their dependents, and civilians working abroad? How many of these are voters?

In 1972, the total number of eligible voters overseas was less than one million. This figure includes about ¾ million members of the armed forces and nearly 200,000 civilians, many of whom are dependents of military personnel stationed abroad. Most are eligible to vote by absentee ballots in their home states.

Do people tend to vote as blocs—for instance, the young, the poor, the blacks, Catholics, Protestants?

Ordinarily, no. With few exceptions, these voters split along lines comparable with the rest of the electorate. The exceptions arise when the special interest of the group is affected in either a positive or negative way, such as in 1964, when well over 90 percent of the blacks voted against Barry Goldwater because they felt threatened in some way by his candidacy. In 1960, a heavy majority of Catholics (many of whom would have otherwise voted for Richard Nixon) supported John F. Kennedy because they identified with him and wanted to help break the Catholic-can't-be-elected view then prevalent in American politics.

What does it mean to "gerrymander" political districts? What's the origin of the word?

The basic meaning is the arrangement of governmental unit boundaries for the benefit of the party in power. The goal is to shape the voting units so that as many of the party's candidates as possible will win election.

For example, a hypothetical city might be 25 percent black. Since 90 percent of the black voters in the city tend to vote Democratic, the Republicans controlling the apportionment, redistricting, or whatever the realignment happens to be, might try to splinter the black vote by chopping up the area and attaching the residual small pieces to separate districts rather than permitting it to remain intact. Such tactics frequently result in unusually shaped political subdivisions and in court suits to overturn the changes.

"Gerrymander" is the combination of a name "Gerry" and the animal "salamander." In 1812, Governor Elbridge Gerry of Massachusetts signed a bill redistricting the state into irregular senatorial districts to the advantage of the Democratic-Republican party, as it was then called. Although he did not sponsor the bill, the Federalist party blamed him for the dragon-like shape of a district in Essex County. The editor of the *Boston Centinel*, a Federalist paper, coined the term for a cartoon executed by the artist Elkanah Tisdale in 1812. There are other versions of who actually used the word first, but it has been in the American political lexicon ever since.

The Gerry-mander.

☞ *A* new species of *Monster*, which appeared in *Essex South District* in January last.

The term "gerrymandering," which means to arrange political boundaries to the advantage of one party over another, resulted from a combination of the name of Governor Elbridge Gerry of Massachusetts and the animal salamander. Artist Elkanah Tisdale drew up the cartoon above for the *Boston Centinel* in 1812 to depict the manner in which Governor Gerry's party had redistricted the state into irregular senatorial districts. *From the Collections of the Library of Congress.*

I've heard a lot about the so-called "Solid South." When did the term originate? Which states does it include?

Although the term "Solid South" did not come into wide political usage until more than a decade after the Civil War, it was used before that to describe eleven former Confederate states which could be counted on to vote as a unit on slavery, states' rights, and similar issues of a sectional nature. The states are Alabama, Arkansas, Florida, Georgia, Louisiana, Mississippi, North Carolina, South Carolina, Tennessee, Texas, and Virginia.

Because Lincoln was a Republican president who had freed the slaves and whose party was in control of the national government during the reconstruction period when the northern carpetbaggers invaded the South, southerners, not surprisingly, turned their allegiance toward the Democratic party. In every election for 40 years, these eleven states gave as a bloc their votes to the Democratic presidential candidate. The first exception was Tennessee in 1920, which voted for Republican Warren G. Harding. In 1924, the South went solidly for the Democratic candidate, but became unglued again in 1928 when five of the eleven states (Florida, North Carolina, Tennessee, Texas, and Virginia) went for Herbert Hoover.

Although the South is still basically Democratic in local elections, it has gone Republican in national and state contests in recent years. In 1952 and again in 1956, Florida, Tennessee, Texas, and Virginia went for Republican Dwight D. Eisenhower, and Republican Richard M. Nixon carried Florida, Tennessee, and Virginia in 1960 against John F. Kennedy. In 1964, Republican Barry Goldwater carried five of the eleven Southern states (Florida, North Carolina, South Carolina, Tennessee, and Virginia), and Richard Nixon carried the same five in 1968.

In short, the Solid South isn't solid anymore. In fact, in his book, *Party Strength in the United States, 1872–1970*, Dr. Paul T. David of the University of Virginia predicts that voting strength between the two major parties will be approximately equal by 1976 if present trends continue.

Which are considered border states?

Chiefly Maryland, Kentucky, and Missouri. Sometimes West Virginia and Oklahoma are added into the border state lineup. Unlike the southern states, these five were never considered part of the solidly Democratic South in presidential elections.

Southern strategy? After GOP presidential candidate Dwight D. Eisenhower carried four southern states in 1952 and in 1956, cartoonist Rube Goldberg came up with this cartoon depicting the Republican party's inroads into the once-solidly Democratic South. *From the Collections of the Library of Congress.*

Where do most of the voters reside—in big cities, the suburbs, or small towns?

The suburbs surrounding large cities contain the biggest single segment of voters (36 percent) followed by the small cities, towns, and farms with 34 percent of the voters. The central cities with populations above fifty thousand have just under 30 percent of the population.

Which states are considered the farm bloc of states?

Iowa, Kansas, Nebraska, North Dakota, and South Dakota.

How many people live on farms?

Just over ten million, or about 5 percent of the total population.

How does the farm vote turn out on election day?

Above average. In 1968, more than 72 percent of voters living on farms went to the polls. The highest rate was among farm owners and managers, whose turnout averaged 80 percent. On the other hand, farm laborers and foremen had a voting rate of just over 50 percent. The black farm vote was well under 50 percent.

How do farmers tend to vote—Republican or Democratic?

In 1968, Richard Nixon received 51 percent of the farm vote, Hubert Humphrey 29 percent, and George Wallace 20 percent. Surveys since then indicate the majority of farmers are still Republican.

What percent of the voters are black? Where are they located?

Slightly over 11 percent are black. The total black population numbers 22.7 million, according to the Census Bureau. Seventy-one percent live in metropolitan centers, making up close to or more than 50 percent of the population in more than two dozen cities, large and small.

Broken down by regions of the country, the South has the biggest black population with 19.2 percent of the total. The Northeast is next with 8.6 percent, and the north central area with 8 percent. The West has the lowest black population with only 4.8 percent.

What's the political party makeup of blacks?

Seventy-four percent of the blacks consider themselves Democrats, 8 percent Republican, and 15 percent independents, according to a 1971 Gallup Poll. Three percent listed other parties or had no opinion.

How does the turnout of black voters compare with white voters?

It is generally lower. In the 1968 presidential election, of the nearly eleven million eligible black voters, an estimated 57 percent actually voted. This compares with a turnout of nearly 69 percent for white voters.

The lowest turnout was by young blacks under twenty-four years of age (35.5 percent) while females between the ages of 45 and 54 had the highest black participation (66.4 percent). As with other categories of voters, the turnout increases as the educational and income level of the voter increases. In fact, according to a survey by the Republican National Committee's Research Division, the highest turnout was recorded by blacks with five or more years of college (90.6 percent). Close behind were whites with five years of college earning $15,000 or over a year (90.1 percent). Next were blacks aged 35–44 making between $10,000 and $15,000 a year (89.6 percent).

How many black elected officials are there in the United States?

Approximately 1,800 including thirteen members of the U.S. House of Representatives and one senator. These figures predate the 1972 elections.

Included in the totals are thirty-three state senators, close to 200 state representatives, about eighty county officials, some sixty mayors or vice-mayors, 650 councilmen or other municipal officials, some 140 judges, and 120 other law enforcement officials, and nearly 500 members of school boards and related offices.

How many women voters are there? Are most of them housewives?

More than half of the nation's voters, nearly 52 percent, are women. Well over 40 percent are employed in jobs outside their homes.

Do women vote for the candidate with the most charisma?

Not necessarily. In the 1960 campaign, John F. Kennedy was considered the presidential candidate with the most charisma. Yet, Richard Nixon carried 51 percent of the female vote that year. In the 1968 election,

THE TWO ADAMS: "IT WAS MY RIB, EVE"

After adoption of the nineteenth amendment to the Constitution, which gave women the right to vote, both political parties claimed credit for the action and both saw new beauty in the fair sex, as depicted in this cartoon by John Knott in the *Dallas Morning News* of August 29, 1920. All together, more than half of the nation's voters—nearly 52 percent—are women. *From the Collections of the Library of Congress.*

however, Hubert Humphrey polled slightly more female support than did Nixon.

In short, women vote pretty much as men do—or vice versa.

How many Americans are there over age sixty-five? Where are they living?

There are twenty million, or 9.9 percent of the total population. The northeastern states have the biggest proportion of elderly (10.6 percent) with the north central states next (10.1 percent), followed by the South (9.6 percent), and the West (8.9 percent).

What is the voting turnout of the elderly? Their party preferences?

Better than the average for the rest of the population. In the 1968 election, 71.5 percent between the ages of 65 and 74 turned out to vote. In that election, Richard Nixon received 47 percent of this group's votes, Hubert Humphrey 41 percent, and George Wallace 12 percent.

What's the religious makeup of voters?

Sixty-eight percent are Protestants, 25 percent Catholics, and 4 percent Jews. Three percent list no religious affiliation.

What about the ethnic background of voters?

This is harder to trace, for several reasons: (1) the U.S. Census Bureau has stopped noting foreign stock after the second generation; (2) inter-marriages make it difficult to classify a family into a particular ethnic category; and (3) ethnic neighborhoods are disappearing as families move into the suburbs.

Despite these facts, millions of Americans still feel deep ethnic ties which influence their voting habits. But as with most voters, these habits cut across regional boundaries and party lines.

How do voters arrive at their political party preference?

Although it was once more significant than today, family tradition is still the single most important factor in determining which of the major parties an individual will be affiliated with. Other influencing factors are peer group, neighborhood, schools attended, race, religion, nationality, occupation, income, and even such seemingly irrelevant items as military service.

Once a voter has made up his mind about his party preference, he tends to stick to it. Adult switches are rarer than you'd think and, when they do occur, are usually from one of the major parties into the independent ranks. Even there, the increase in the number of voters who classified themselves as independent rose only 6 percent between 1940 and 1970.

After enactment in 1970 of the constitutional amendment granting the vote to youngsters eighteen and above, the number of voters classifying themselves as independents increased another 4 percent as a majority of first-time voters (52 percent) classified themselves as independents.

One survey, conducted by Robert D. Hess and Judith V. Torney and titled *The Development of Political Attitudes in Children*, reports that by age ten, which is usually the fifth grade, more than one half of all children consider themselves as little Republicans or little Democrats. In an article by M. Kent Jennings and Richard G. Niemi in the *American Political Science Review*, called "Transmission of Political Values from Parent to Child," the authors contend that, among parents who identify with one party or the other, there is a better than even chance that the child will adopt the same party by age seventeen.

Okay, but do the youngsters really understand why they belong to one party or the other?

In most cases, no. In his book, *The American Party System and the American People*, Fred I. Greenstein declares, "For the young child, party identification is so barren of supporting information that he may be able to say, 'I am a Republican,' or 'I am a Democrat' without even knowing the party of the incumbent president." Greenstein cited one study he had made which found that it is not until the seventh grade that even a few children start to differentiate between the parties in terms of what they stand for. Adds Greenstein, "Some adults—but only a very few—manage to stay in this state of blissful ignorance."

What's meant by the term "one man, one vote"?

In defining the political boundaries for state legislative seats and congressional districts, "one man, one vote" means that the states must draw the lines to attain as nearly as possible an equality of population among the districts. In other words, such disparities as one legislative district containing three times the population of another in the same state have been ruled out.

The requirement stemmed from a 1962 Supreme Court decision in the case of *Baker v. Carr* which held that the lower house of the Tennessee Legislature must be apportioned solely on the basis of population. In a similar ruling, the Supreme Court held in the 1964 case of *Wesberry v. Sanders* that congressional districts must be composed of substantially equal numbers of people. Another 1964 decision, *Reynolds v. Sims,* held that both houses of bicameral legislative districts must be "as nearly of equal population as practicable."

Once I'm registered to vote, am I eligible as long as I remain a resident of the state I'm living in?

Your continuing eligibility varies by states. For instance, two states, Alaska and North Dakota, have no requirement for registration; nine will keep you on the books permanently once you've registered, even though you don't actually go to the polls; nine others require you to vote in every general election to keep your eligibility current; nine states require that you vote at least once every four years to keep your name on the registration list; six will keep you on their voting lists if you have voted once in any election in the two preceding years; three states require you to have voted in one of the two preceding general elections; three others insist that you vote in every primary and general election to maintain eligibility; two states require you to vote at least once during a five-year period to remain enrolled, one state every six years, and so forth. In other words, since requirements vary so markedly, check your local laws.

Do persons convicted of crimes lose the right to vote? If so, for how long?

Maine is the only state whose laws do not contain some provisions for disfranchising persons convicted of certain crimes, according to a 1967 study published by the Library of Congress. Usually the crimes for which conviction includes loss of the right to vote are felonies, treason, crimes of moral turpitude, and generally those considered infamous or serious which are punishable by long prison terms. However, there are exceptions, notably Massachusetts and Vermont, where disfranchisement results only for the commission of certain crimes relating to the electoral process.

Regaining the right to vote depends in most cases upon the convict obtaining a pardon from the governor. In several states—Colorado, Delaware, Hawaii, Illinois, Michigan, Minnesota, New York, Oregon, and Wisconsin—the right to vote is regained automatically upon completion of sentence. In a handful of others, conviction of certain crimes, usually those related to the electoral process, brings with it the loss of the right to vote for specific, usually short, periods of time. In Massachusetts, for instance, voting rights are restored automatically three years after loss due to conviction for an election-related offense. In Vermont, the loss is restricted to the election to which the crime was related.

Congress has shown some interest in legislation to restore voting rights, at least in federal elections, to convicted felons who have completed their sentences. However, the issue is muddied somewhat because such federal enactments would involve Congress further in the matter of establishing voter qualifications, a power which generally has been reserved to the states.

Where do the words vote and voter come from?

The word "vote" is derived from the Latin *votum*, which means "vow" or "wish." The term was first used in Great Britain in the sixteenth century to indicate the casting of a ballot. A voter is simply the follow-up term indicating the person who casts the ballot.

I've heard the old expression, "Vote early and often." Just what does it mean?

In the early days of the country, before registration was required, hired voters would roam from one voting precinct to another, voting over and over again. The admonition to party workers to vote early and often became as well used a phrase as the "tombstone vote" did later on. In that case, deceased voters were kept on registration lists long after they passed away, and ballots were cast in their names on election day. Tighter registration laws and poll-watchers have sharply curtailed this type of election-day activity.

How was the first Tuesday in November chosen as election day?

Actually it's not the first Tuesday—it's the first Tuesday after the first Monday in November, as specified by legislation passed by Congress and signed into law on January 23, 1845, by President John Tyler.

Since the Constitution provided that Congress set the election date, the legislators decided on the first Tuesday after the first Monday as a result of a number of compromises. Monday was ruled out because in those days many voters had to start for the polls the day before the election to make it, and many objected to travelling on Sunday. The first Tuesday in November was excluded because it might fall on the first of the month and inconvenience people in business. The second Tuesday was ruled out because it could fall too close to the first Wednesday in December, which an earlier Congress had decreed as the date the electors were to meet and cast their ballots.

CHAPTER 5

What makes a successful campaign?

What are the chief ingredients of a winning campaign?

There are several basic ingredients. Although not necessarily in the order of importance, they include (1) an attractive and articulate candidate; (2) ample funds to carry out the basic objectives of the campaign; (3) competent management to make sure the campaign is conducted as professionally as possible; (4) good public relations and publicity to carry the candidate's message to the voters; (5) effective precinct organization to pinpoint the candidate's vote and to get it to the polls; and (6) issues which can be used to advantage.

How important is the campaign in influencing the outcome of an election?

Very important. Since approximately one-third of the voters make up their minds in the weeks just before the election, the campaign is the candidate's chief way to reach and influence them, to enlist their support behind his candidacy, to shore up their views and attitudes about him, and to arouse fears and concerns about his opponent. In short, the campaign is ordinarily what makes the difference between victory and defeat.

What are the best ways to reach voters in a campaign?

There are four chief methods:

1. Personal contact—carrying the campaign to the people in walking tours of towns and cities; shaking hands with voters and passing out campaign folders, pamphlets, or other speciality items; meeting with workers at local plants as shifts change; attending meetings, conferences and rallies.

2. Publicity activities—making news which will be carried in the newspapers and over radio and television about the campaign and its activities.

3. Advertising—buying space in newspapers and other publications and on billboards, and buying time on radio and TV to sell voters on the candidate.

4. Direct mail—including personal letters to friends and supporters, campaign postcards, brochures, and other literature, all designed to reach the voter through his mailbox and convince him to vote the "right" way.

Which of the above four is the most effective method of campaigning?

They're all important. However, keep in mind that in a single radio or television appearance, a candidate will reach more voters than he will personally be able to meet and shake hands with during his entire compaign. For that reason, an appearance on radio or TV should take precedence over a handshaking tour or a civic luncheon speech in scheduling the candidate.

Who are the best campaign workers?

Women are, by far. In his book, *Winning Your Campaign,* Hank Parkinson tells candidates for office that "one good woman is worth three men in any campaign," adding, "The guys are usually just too busy making a living to give you the amount of time you need, or their talents can be better used in other areas—fund-raising, on the speaker's bureau and in contacts with other businessmen. Women can broaden your base of citizen support, increase contacts with additional potential voters and handle the mountain of detail that accompanies any campaign."

What kind of planning goes into a campaign? I have always heard that campaigns are structured on a master plan or grand strategy aimed at "peaking" just before the election. True?

Actually, a successful campaign requires a carefully laid out battle plan aimed at effecting maximum exposure for the candidate and his views and optimum turnout of voters favorable to him on election day. However, it doesn't always work that way.

As former Democratic National Chairman Lawrence O'Brien put it in an interview with columnist John P. Roche, "You start a campaign with a plan, with everything laid out, and then 'bang'—something you never dreamed of happens. Within a month, nobody but Teddy White remembers that you had a plan." (White is the author of *Making of the President*.)

Reminiscing about John F. Kennedy's 1960 presidential primaries campaign, O'Brien said that everyone came around after the West Virginia election which Kennedy, who was a Catholic, won, congratulating him on his courage in entering a solidly Protestant state and praising his wisdom in winning. "Actually," he said, "if anyone had urged Jack to go into West Virginia, he should have been thrown down the stairs. . . . We were trapped."

O'Brien summed up: "A master political strategist is somebody who wins an election—even if he doesn't know how he did it. He can then read the columns and find out the secret of his success."

As far as peaking a campaign is concerned, it usually refers to maximizing the candidate's energies and his resources so that the campaign is at its peak on election eve. This requires directing all efforts, including free publicity, paid advertising, direct mail, and the candidate's scheduling, toward reaching the maximum number of voters possible in a favorable way immediately before they go to the polls. Candidates often become concerned about peaking their campaigns too soon, which usually puts them on the downslide at election time.

What's the difference between the terms "canvass" and "campaign"?

The term "campaign" is an updated version of the early "canvass," first used in British elections to refer to the preelection contest. "Campaign" caught on in this country in the early 1800s as politicians made comparisons between a political canvass and a military campaign, and combined the two into the phrase political campaign.

The comparison between military and political activities was succinctly stressed by Sen. John J. Ingalls, Republican president pro tempore of the U.S. Senate, in an interview with the *New York World* in 1890. He said:

Politics is a battle for supremecy. Parties are the armies. The Decalogue and the Golden Rule have no place in a political campaign. The object is success. To defeat the antagonist and expel the party in power is the purpose. The Republicans and Democrats are as irrevocably opposed to each other as were Grant and Lee in the

Wilderness. They use ballots instead of guns, but the struggle is as unrelenting and desperate and the result sought for the same.

More recently, the term canvass has taken on the connotation of surveying the voters in advance of an election to ascertain their sentiment on an candidate or an issue.

What's meant by the term "grass roots"? Where did it start?

It's a descriptive way of identifying basic public attitudes, the views and opinions of the so-called rank-and-file voters. The term is believed to have been first used in the political sense in the early 1900s and is in common use today in national politics. Congressmen frequently will say they are returning to their home districts to sample grass roots thinking.

The keynoter at the Bull Moose Convention in 1912, Indiana Sen. Albert J. Beveridge, employed the term in his speech when he said, "This party comes from the grass roots. It has grown from the soil of the people's hard necessities." Calvin Coolidge put it this way in the 1920s: "The real test of party strength is down close to the grass roots."

When is the best time to start running for office? When is the best time to publicly announce such a decision?

First off, the candidate should start running from the moment he makes the decision to do so. When he announces this decision publicly is another matter.

Ordinarily, it is best to announce early, to be the first candidate in the field. For one thing, an early announcement may help to scare others off from entering the race, give the candidate first crack at contributors' money that is available, and enable him to line up commitments for support before other candidates do so.

There are disadvantages, of course, to an early announcement. If the candidate has a ready-made platform for public appearances, such as being a member of a local commission or organization prominent in the news, an early announcement of candidacy may shut off speaking invitations. Also, a long, drawn-out campaign can tax his funds and energies to the point where both are lacking when needed in the immediate preelection stretch.

Generally speaking, however, this rule of thumb applies: a newcomer to politics should announce his candidacy sufficiently early to enable him to become known to his potential constituency and to build up his organization and treasury for the campaign itself. This usually means announcing from six months to a year before the election.

How important is the timing of an announcement of candidacy?

Like just about everything else in a campaign, timing is important to success, sometimes even vital. In making an announcement of candidacy, it is important to strive for a time when it will obtain maximum coverage in the newspapers and over radio and television so that voters will notice it. Holiday periods should be avoided since people are either away or preoccupied. Deadline day announcements should also be avoided as there is usually a last-minute rush, and the event may be buried in an overall story and lose much of its impact. Weekend announcements are also bad, because voters seem to watch less television news and read their newspapers less carefully.

Ordinarily, Monday is the best day to announce, because it's a slow news day. The time of day should be governed by the type of newspapers in the area. If there are heavy-circulation afternoon newspapers, a Monday morning announcement may provide the best P.M. coverage in these papers. This will also provide TV stations with ample time to film and edit the story for evening news use. If there are heavy-circulation morning newspapers, aim for an afternoon announcement. This will still provide ample time for TV use that evening and will give the news break to the better-read morning papers. In short, to obtain maximum exposure, consider the convenience of the media in scheduling an announcement, whether it be at a press conference or a simple declaration of candidacy in the form of a news release which is distributed to the media.

What's the first and most important rule a candidate for office must adhere to?

Work like hell. If the candidate doesn't, the rest of his crew isn't likely to either.

An equally important rule is that the candidate should not serve as his own campaign manager. He has enough to do merely being the contender. This doesn't mean he is prohibited from making inputs or developing strategy. However, he should stay out of the day-to-day, nuts-and-bolts administration of the effort. Nothing leads to a dissipation of the candidate's energies and efforts more quickly. If he's sitting in the campaign headquarters arranging his schedule, who's out meeting the voters?

What is the role of the candidate's wife in the campaign? How can she be most helpful to her husband?

There are any number of ways in which a wife can contribute to her husband's political success. For example, she can campaign directly for him. One candidate's wife made an extensive impact by going door to door with a "little red wagon" loaded with campaign brochures.

She can carry the candidate's message to women's groups, sorority meetings, coffee and tea sessions. She can accompany the candidate to functions and divide the physical problem of meeting large numbers of people personally.

In short, a wife's role largely varies with the availability of her time and talents. One caution, however, is to avoid the image of the wife abandoning the family, especially if the couple has a large number of children, by too-extensive participation.

I've heard it said that selling political candidates and soap is similar. Is this true?

There are similarities and differences. Taking the similarities first, there's the brand name, which, in the case of politics, is the political party. Then there's the label—what the party stands for and what its platform says about it. Finally, there's the product itself, the candidate.

In politics, the voters are the buyers, and if they don't like the merchandise or the way it performs, they'll change brands at the next election. And the best sales campaign in the world won't help.

Unlike soap, however, the candidate is a live, walking, talking human being, with all the failings and hangups of human beings, which means he can unglue the best-laid campaign plans by an ill-chosen comment or an untoward action. Take the case of the congressional candidate who referred to his opponent in a speech as a "hired hand" because he had worked for others all his life and had never met a payroll himself. The opposing candidate, well aware that there are more employees than employers, immediately pounced on the phrase, turning it to his advantage. Almost overnight, billboards, newspaper ads, radio and TV commercials, and direct mailings inundated the district with his newly bequeathed slogan, "Let me be your hired hand in Washington." The voters let him.

What about the "packaging" of candidates which I've heard so much about? How is this done?

Actually, the packaging concept is a somewhat pejorative term which, translated, simply means the most effective use of the techniques of advertising to sell the candidate and his views to the voter.

The packaging notion, comment Richard Scammon and Ben Wattenberg in *The Real Majority*, "concerns how many millions of dollars were spent on television time, how the video tape was spliced to make the candidate look better than he was—and so on. What else is new?" The two authors noted that Caesar brought grain from North Africa to the citizens of Rome to influence an election; that an intellectual, introspective lawyer from Springfield made points with the electorate as "Honest Abe the Rail Splitter"; that Mark Hanna packaged presidential aspirant William McKinley by keeping him on his front porch in Canton, Ohio, talking face to face with Americans who came to visit from all over the country, because McKinley couldn't compete as an orator with his opponent, William Jennings Bryan.

"Of course candidates are packaged," say the two authors. "Most people are packaged—psychiatrists call it role playing."

What's meant by image?

Although it's an overworked term, image is still the simplest way to describe what the candidate projects to the voters—how they view him as an individual and assess his philosophy as a politician. The best candidate image is one of a warm human being, fully cognizant of the responsibilities of the office he is seeking and confident of his ability to meet them. He should project concern about the problems of his constituency and determination to do something about them.

Since voters tend to cast their ballots for a candidate whom they either know or know something favorable about, it is important that the image they hold of him in their minds be a positive one. Although a good image won't necessarily assure a candidate's election, a negative one will go a long way toward defeating him.

One point to keep in mind is that, although public relations and publicity techniques can help to shape and project a candidate's image to the voters, they can't remake him into something he isn't. They can't turn an unattractive and inarticulate individual into a spellbinding matinee idol, in short. The candidate has to inherently have the basic qualities to begin with, which the image makers can then project into public view.

What exactly do you mean by public relations? And is publicity the same as public relations?

There are about as many definitions of public relations as people who practice the art. For political purposes, however, the term can best be defined as the development of a well-rounded program to project the candidate for office and his views to the voters in the best possible light through newspapers, radio and television, and related means.

Publicity, on the other hand, is one of the tools of public relations used in building the candidate's image. Let's say, for instance, that a candidate for commissioner of roads decides upon a public relations strategy aimed at depicting himself as a man of action who gets things done, and his opponent as a do-nothing incumbent. In developing publicity situations tied into this theme, he might appear in coveralls in front of his home with a shovel, filling up the potholes in the street which his opponent had obviously neglected. A photo in the local newspaper and a newsclip on TV is the kind of exposure that could result.

What about advertising? Where does it fit in?

First, let's redefine our terms in this way. When the candidate creates news to promote his candidacy and obtains free space in the news columns of papers and free time on radio and TV newscasts, that's public relations, or, more specifically, publicity. When he buys space in publications and time on radio and television to sell his candidacy, that's advertising. Usage of the latter is guaranteed because it's bought and paid for whereas the former isn't.

Which is more important—advertising or public relations?

Both are important to a campaign. Because the candidate controls the timing of advertising, he is able to place ads in newspapers, commercials on radio and TV, and send out direct mailing pieces to pace the campaign toward its peak—ideally, on election eve. At the same time, public relations is important in establishing credibility for the candidate by obtaining free exposure for him in the news media. By a rough rule of thumb, a half column of favorable news is worth a half page of purchased advertising in the same paper, and a minute of favorable exposure on the nighttime TV news is worth ten one-minute, paid commercials on the same station.

What's the best way to get news about the campaign to the media?

Although there are a number of ways, the simplest is through what is called the news release. Basically, the release is nothing more than a short, to-the-point summary of what the candidate is doing or saying, written like a news story. Since it is often the only regular contact the candidate and his organization have with news outlets, the release should be prepared professionally in both style and content, for this is what shapes opinion in the minds of editors, writers, or broadcasters about the candidate and his campaign. And news coverage ordinarily increases in proportion to the professionalism of this activity.

Is there a secret for getting news coverage during a campaign?

Yes. Make sure everything the candidate does and says in an effort to obtain coverage is newsworthy.

Just what is a newsworthy story which the press might pick up and use?

The possibilities run the gamut from legitimate campaign announcements, in which, for example, the candidate lists the appointment of key campaign personnel or announces his speaking schedule, to speeches outlining his own programs or attacking those of his opponent. Publicity ploys devised by the candidate to obtain news coverage also run the gamut. For instance, in a recent election, a congressional candidate attacked his incumbent opponent as an absentee congressman who neglected his constituents and didn't even own a home in the district he represented. Finally, the incumbent responded in a statement to the press that he did, indeed, have a home in the congressional district, and listed its address. The challenger checked the address and found the home was titled to the congressman, but that it was vacant and for rent. So he rented it for his campaign headquarters! The ensuing publicity helped defeat the incumbent.

Is it possible for a candidate to be overexposed in the media?

Yes, if it's the wrong kind of exposure. News stories in which the candidate is constantly quoted in favor of a position opposed by a majority of voters are an example. Also, if a candidate isn't telegenic, he should be kept off TV, and if he has a poor speaking voice, he should avoid radio as well. Exposure of this kind hurts more than it helps.

But given an attractive candidate with a pleasing voice and personality and with views in accord with his constituency, there's no such thing as overexposure, particularly if he's trying to unseat an incumbent. If the candidate is capable of making news daily, especially in the closing weeks of a campaign, more power to him.

In fact, constant repetition of the candidate's name and message on the minds of the voters, whether through paid advertising or free publicity, is vital to the reinforcement of his image to the electorate. According to one survey, a message has to be repeated seventeen times before it starts to really sink into the average citizen's mind.

I once heard a politician say to a reporter, "I don't care what you say about me as long as you spell my name right." What did he mean? Is that the way most officeholders feel?

No. It's a fatuous old cliché whose roots are indeterminate, perhaps stemming from New York's Tammany Hall around the turn of the century.

The essence of the statement is that the politician feels that people either don't remember what they read or don't care. On that basis, his only concern is that they remember his name so they will recognize it when they go to the polls.

These days, the politician who holds this view doesn't last long in office. In fact, bad publicity has too often resulted in an incumbent's ouster from office at the next election, which is why he cares very much what the news media write and say about him and why he seeks to build and maintain the best possible public image of himself.

What's the best way of determining which issues are important in a campaign?

The best way is to have a poll made by a professional organization which specializes in surveys of this kind. Using scientific techniques and an adequate sample of voters, such a survey will provide the candidate with up-to-date and accurate information on what people actually think— not what he *thinks* they think. This information can aid the candidate not only in determining issues which are troubling voters but in assessing his own strengths and weaknesses and those of his opponent.

How much does such a poll cost?

Depends upon the size of the population you want sampled and upon the firm making the survey. The average poll runs roughly $10 per voter surveyed. In a congressional district, for instance, a representative sampling would consist of approximately 400 voters and would cost between $4,000 and $5,000; in a statewide race, between $10,000 and $15,000.

What if a candidate can't afford to have a poll made? How can he obtain information on how he's running and on issues?

Even though some pollsters may tell you it's unscientific, there is a simple yet highly effective way of determining voter sentiment. It's called the "Supermarket Poll" and has been used with great success by a number of candidates.

Developed by Charles G. Kerch of San Diego, the supermarket poll has been proven accurate within 3 percent over the years, which closely rivals the margin of error in the Gallup and Harris polls. Basically, it works like this: volunteers canvass supermarkets, usually on weekends, asking voters their preferences on competing candidates and even their views on major issues.

How do I go about setting up such a poll?

Here are some basic pointers:

1. In using volunteers, make sure they are trained to keep their own personal views out of the questions asked. The inflection of the voice or facial expression when asking a question can often influence the reply and distort the findings.

2. Conduct the polls in large supermarkets which will provide a better cross section of voters from the area—men as well as women, persons on welfare as well as the wealthy, those walking as well as driving, etc. The questions should be asked before the customers enter the store, not when they're leaving with bags full of groceries.

3. The polls should be conducted on Saturday, since this is a day which brings out a better cross section of voters. Generally, 90 percent of those asked to respond will take the time to do so, since Saturday shopping is usually a leisurely affair.

4. This approach is suggested for volunteers contacting voters: "This

is a political poll. If you were voting today for [title of office], would you vote for [list the candidates, rotating the order of their names to assure that respondees aren't simply agreeing to the first name mentioned]?" It is usually best to start with the presidential, gubernatorial, or congressional races first and ask about local races last.

5. If you want a sounding on issues, the same approach can be used, posing the question as objectively as possible. For instance, an open-ended question: "What do you think is the most important problem facing this country [or city, county, or town] today?" Or on a specific issue: "Do you favor or oppose the busing of Negro and white school children from one school district to another?"

6. The final question should be: "Are you registered Republican or Democrat?" Don't ask this one until all other questions are asked, however. The actual percentage of votes a Republican candidate can win from Democratic voters is just as important to know as the percentage a GOP candidate can lose from Republicans who defect from his candidacy and vice versa, of course. It's also important to know how many voters are undecided on any given race or issue.

7. If you want to broaden your sampling, use more persons, each at a large supermarket in various parts of your district. Each interviewer should obtain a minimum of 25–50 samples which, if conducted each Saturday, will provide an excellent broad-based summary of the popularity of the candidates and voters' feeling on crucial issues.

8. After the results of one thousand interviews are in, they should be compared in lots of one hundred with the succeeding hundred. If the results of each match, or closely so, then the survey can be relied upon. Normally, you will get only one bad survey out of ten.

How many persons do pollsters such as Gallup and Harris contact to obtain their results?

Ordinarily, the Gallup and Harris organizations use a sampling of 1,500 persons across the country in determining a national attitude on major issues. Using the latest U.S. Census Bureau data, these 1,500 are selected to conform to a representative cross section of the adult civilian population living in private households (excluding persons in institutions, hospitals, or on military posts). If a larger sampling is required—for instance, to project the winner in a presidential contest—the pollsters usually double or triple this number to reduce the sampling error.

How reliable are pollsters like Gallup and Harris in predicting elections?

If properly conducted, with a representative sampling of the electorate, a poll can provide an accurate measurement of voter sentiment on the election at the time it is made. The problem is that voters are asked how they would ballot if the election were held today, not how they intend to vote on election day or even if they intend to vote at all. This gives the pollster something of an out, if his results go awry. He can claim a shift in voter sentiment after his sampling was made or in the closing days of the campaign. And sometimes this shift does take place.

Although I read a lot about polls in the newspapers, I have never been asked my opinion, nor have I ever met anyone who was contacted. How can these polls really be accurate?

Since only 1,500 persons are interviewed nationwide in any given poll, which is only a tiny part of the population, the laws of probability are that you won't be interviewed in your lifetime. Dr. George Gallup explains it this way: "It has been estimated that a poll of 100 million adults of the nation—even if that poll reached 10,000 persons weekly—would require 500 years to get around to each person."

Can a candidate rely on his friends for reliable soundings on how he's doing?

Usually not. The problem is that the candidate's friends too often tell him what he wants to hear rather than what he should hear. They provide him with well-intentioned but bad information, in other words.

How and when did political polling start in this country?

Although the use of political polls dates back nearly 150 years, they have come into their own as effective campaign tools only in recent years. A check of historical records turns up one straw poll taken by a Pennsylvania newspaper in the 1824 presidential election campaign. It showed Andrew Jackson running ahead of John Quincy Adams, a sounding which turned out to be correct as Jackson won a popular plurality, although he lost to Adams when the election was thrown into the House of Representatives. Other newspapers and publications conducted straw polls throughout the last century and into this one, with scientific surveying techniques coming into use to replace the earlier discredited methods in the late 1940s and early 1950s.

Is it possible for polls not only to measure public opinion but also to influence it as well, by the release of results which show one candidate with a substantial lead over another?

Although this "bandwagon" theory has been often raised during election campaigns, it usually isn't proven out by the results on election day. In fact, there are innumerable examples of candidates leading in early polls who subsequently dropped in later ones or even lost in the final balloting. Take Richard Nixon's early campaign lead of 15 percent over Hubert Humphrey in 1968, a lead which was finally translated into a Nixon victory by less than 1 percent. Or take an even better example: the near-unanimous projection by pollsters and pundits of Thomas E. Dewey's election in 1948 by a big margin over President Harry S Truman.

In short, if the bandwagon theory had substance, both Nixon and Dewey would have won overwhelmingly as voters clambered aboard to be with the winner. More likely, what happened was a reverse bandwagon psychology—namely, that supporters of the trailing candidate as well as the candidate himself were stirred to greater efforts, and supporters of the leading candidate became complacent, resulting in the closing of the gap between the two.

Where did the word "bandwagon" come from?

Although not widely used until about 1900, the term probably originated in the 1840 campaign of William Henry Harrison. His Whig supporters made great use of a bandwagon at the head of their parades. In it rode local candidates as well as the band. People who wanted to be identified with the candidate attempted to climb on the vehicle while those who were less enthusiastic merely walked behind.

The term is used more in relation to political rather than nonpolitical events. It appears with the greatest frequency in the media quadrennially just before and during the presidential primaries and nominating conventions.

Who said, "Politics has gotten so expensive it even takes a lot of money to get beat with"?

The late Will Rogers said it. And he was so right.

How much does it take to get elected president these days? U.S. senator? Congressman? Governor of a state?

By best estimates, close to $400 million is spent on campaigns in a major election year such as 1972. This includes the funds of well over a quarter of a million candidates seeking offices from the presidency on down to the local school board and town clerk.

Ordinarily, the incumbent has the advantage in running against a challenger. At the national level, this includes free mailing privileges, free staff paid for by the taxpayers, and a range of free services and assistance which he can use to make points with his constituents—not to mention the free forum for publicity which his office provides. For these reasons, a challenger will usually have to spend more on his campaign to overcome the built-in advantage of the incumbent.

At the presidential level, it can cost from $35 million on up for a candidate to win his party's nomination and conduct a winning campaign. According to Dr. Herbert E. Alexander in *Financing Parties and Campaigns in 1968*, Richard Nixon spent an estimated $8.5 million in his campaign for the Republican nomination, and his party then spent another $28 million to get him elected. His opponent, Hubert Humphrey, and the Democratic party spent about half this amount, Dr. Alexander says.

Depending on the size of the state, a challenger for the U.S. Senate can spend from $250,000 to $5 million, including costs of a primary. Similar figures apply to a gubernatorial campaign.

The cost of campaigning for the U.S. House of Representatives is somewhat less but still expensive. If you include a contested primary, costs can range up as high as $300,000 in some districts. The average House primary contest costs between $15,000 and $30,000 and the general campaign between $60,000 and $80,000 in a rural area, and between $100,000 and $125,000 in an urban area.

Is there a major campaign advantage to being an incumbent?

Yes indeed. The fact that close to 90 percent of all incumbents seeking reelection make it is a pretty good indication of the advantages of already being in office. For one thing, the incumbent is usually not only better known, but has the forum and facilities of his office as a platform for publicity and a vehicle for reaching voters. And that's an advantage that most challengers aren't able to overcome.

What have the spending levels been in recent years for presidential campaigns? Is there an upward trend?

The spending levels indeed have been going up in what is clearly a trend.

In the 1968 presidential campaign, at least $49,260,000 was spent for the three major candidates. Through their own campaign committees, the Republicans spent $28,848,000 in behalf of Richard Nixon, the Democrats $13,169,000 for Hubert H. Humphrey, and the American Independent party $7,243,000 for George C. Wallace. Other groups added $4,121,-000 to that total.

The 1964 estimate was $34,788,000, compared with $25,014,000 in 1960, and $17,200,000 in 1956, reflecting a tripling of the spending level in the space of a dozen years.

How about campaign spending overall? Is that on the increase as well?

Yes. The 1952 expenditures estimate for offices at all levels was $140 million; for 1956, it was $155 million, and for 1960, it was $175 million. By 1964, the level had risen to $200 million, and by 1968 to $300 million.

Interestingly, while the cost per vote has increased also, as might be expected, campaign spending expressed as a percentage of Gross National Product has declined, according to a study by Howard R. Penniman which was published by American Enterprise Institute for Public Policy Research in 1971. He reported:

> When measured against the number of voters in each of the years, these expenditures show large increases in the cost per vote cast. When compared against Gross National Product, however, the increase in campaign spending fades away. The 1952 expenditure amounted to .04 percent of GNP. In the years since then, the tremendous growth in campaign expenses has been more than offset by the more rapid growth in GNP, so that the 1968 expenditure amounted to .035 percent of GNP for that year.

Dr. Herbert E. Alexander of the Citizens Research Foundation has sought to put the matter of campaign expenditures in perspective. While political parties at all levels spent $300 million in 1968, he notes, Procter and Gamble alone spent $275 million that year to advertise its products.

Why are campaign spending levels going up? Is it primarily television?

The figures would seem to bear this out.

In 1956, the television expenditure for political advertising was $6,636,-000 compared with $27,087,000 in 1968, according to the Twentieth Century Fund Commission on Costs in the Electronic Era. The number of television sets more than doubled in that time from less than 38 million to more than 84 million, located in 95 percent of American homes. As the viewing audience grew, so did advertising rates. Another cost factor which must be considered, of course, is inflation.

How expensive are primary elections for presidential candidates?

Very. In 1968, the aspirants spent close to $40 million in slightly more than twelve states, according to Dr. Herbert E. Alexander in *Financing Parties and Campaigns in 1968*.

The highest expenditures were recorded by Robert Kennedy and Eugene McCarthy. The two senators totalled $9 million each in those primaries, followed by Richard Nixon, $8.5 million; Nelson Rockefeller, $7 million; Hubert Humphrey, $4 million; George Romney, $1.5 million; Ronald Reagan, a "noncandidate," $800,000; President Johnson, $500,000; Sen. George McGovern, $100,000; and Harold Stassen, $90,000.

Interestingly, the money spent in the Democratic presidential primaries in 1968 exceeded the total amount Hubert Humphrey had available for his general election campaign.

How about campaign expenditures? Is there a yardstick covering how much to spend?

Although campaign expenditures vary sharply with the office sought and size of the constituency, a rough rule of thumb used by many professionals is $1.00 per vote. But there are so many exceptions that it isn't really much of a rule to go by.

How can you tell how much to spend on radio and TV commercials?

You can never be sure. As the late George Washington Hill, president of the American Tobacco Company, once said, "Fifty percent of my advertising is wasted, but I don't know which 50 percent."

More succinctly, Henry R. Howell, Lieutenant Governor of Virginia,

The high cost of campaigning, particularly on television, was pointed up by this Temple cartoon. Even with the 1972-enacted Federal Election Campaign Act, which set ceilings on media spending, the cost of running for public office is still out of sight for most political aspirants. *From the Collections of the Library of Congress.*

put it this way when asked about how many TV commercials a candidate should purchase in a campaign: "It's the old butterbean story again. If it takes 1,000 butterbeans to make the water flow over the bathtub, there's no use dropping in four. All you do is waste four perfectly good butter-beans."

In a study of broadcast use in the 1970 congressional campaigns, Paul Dawson and James Zinser concluded in *Public Opinion Quarterly* that winning candidates for the U.S. House of Representatives spent an average of $6,200 on radio and television (or an average of about $.09 per voter) and winning Senate candidates spent an average of $123,500 (or $.24 per voter).

Can you suggest some simple do's and don'ts of campaigning?

Yes, here are an even dozen never and always suggestions:

1. Never equivocate or use "weasel words"; always make your position clear.

2. Never try to bluff through on a subject you don't know about; always do your homework, become informed, state your opinion, and have the facts to back it up.

3. Never be afraid to say "I don't know"; always say, "but I'll find out."

4. Never be afraid to ask for help; always call for assistance. (You'll need it, too.)

5. Never try to do everything yourself; always pick your people carefully, then make them responsible for details while you tend to the business of campaigning.

6. Never try to spread yourself too thin; always schedule your appearances so that you have time to prepare for them—even allow for transportation foul-ups.

7. Never desert your own party; always use it as a base of support to attract members of the opposite party.

8. Never mislead or lie to the press; always be candid, but don't hesitate to say "no comment."

9. Never promise the world in order to get cooperation or support; always be considerate of others' interests, but make only commitments you can fill after the election.

10. Never personally take money for your campaign; always have a full-time money-raiser who is capable of handling your campaign finances, filling out reports, and tapping a wide scope of contribution sources.

Political name-calling provoked this cartoon by Reg Manning in which he depicts the animals as fighting back. Manning titled it: "Can't Say We Blame 'Em." Political smears are a variation of this tactic and usually backfire on the candidate originating the charge. On occasion, interestingly, the spreading of a *true* statement about a person in public life can be considered a smear. *From the Collections of the Library of Congress.*

11. Never cross the line between humility and arrogance; always be a nice guy.

12. Never talk too much; always smile a lot.

What's a political smear? Where did the term start?

The term means the employment of irresponsible charges which are likely to damage the reputation of either a person or an organization or hold it up to public contempt. The term was first used in England in the sense of greasing, smudging, or tarnishing someone's reputation.

What can a candidate do about a smear?

He has several choices: (1) he can ignore it entirely; (2) he can counter-attack on the theory that a good offense is the best defense; (3) he can indignantly deny it; (4) he can take the edge off the charge by admitting it beforehand, if it happens to be true and if he knows it is coming; (5) he can offer a reward if his opponent can prove the charges are true; or (6) he can file a complaint of unfair tactics against his opponent with the Fair Campaign Practices Committee in Washington.

What's the best course, usually?

Depends. Unless the smear is actually hurting the candidate's election chances, the best course is to ignore it. A few years back the Democrats accused Richard Nixon, who was then vice-president under Dwight D. Eisenhower, of having called Harry Truman a traitor. GOP National Chairman Leonard Hall ended the discussion by offering a reward if the Democrats could show where Nixon had made the charge against Truman.

How about the Fair Campaign Practices Committee? Could it help in such a case?

Not much, really. The committee has a small staff in Washington and no investigators in the field to check into complaints filed with it. Usually a candidate will file a complaint about his opponent's tactics with the committee for the publicity value he can get out of it. The committee then asks the opponent to respond, usually within three days, to the charges against him. The committee then makes public the original charge and the denial without making a determination as to who's right and who's wrong.

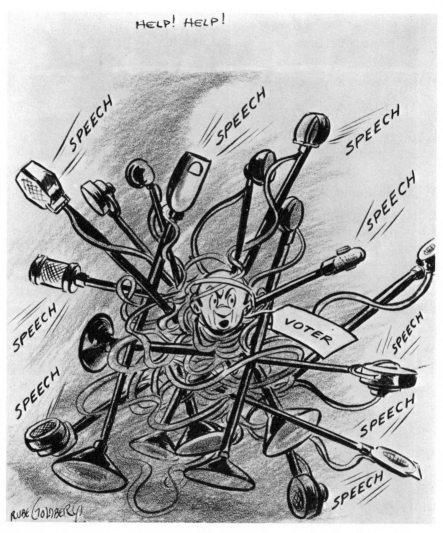

Ghost-to-ghost hookup? After being inundated with election year speeches, most voters probably feel like cartoonist Rube Goldberg's man, shown above calling for "Help!" Most candidates for major public offices employ "ghost writers" to research and prepare speeches for their use; some even use humor writers to lighten up their talks with topical one-liners. *From the Collections of the Library of Congress.*

What if the smear happens to be true? In other words, can truth be a smear?

In a sense, yes. William Safire, in his book *The New Language of Politics*, notes that during the infighting for the Democratic presidential nomination in 1960, Sen. Lyndon B. Johnson's supporters claimed that Sen. John F. Kennedy was a victim of Addison's disease which required regular cortisone treatment. The Kennedy forces, however, admitted that their man had only "a mild adrenal deficiency."

However, Safire reports that an article in the *Journal of the American Medical Association* in 1967 "rather conclusively substantiated the original charge." Adds Safire, "Nevertheless, most politicians consider the original attack a smear; while truth may be a legal defense against libel, the spreading of a damaging story about a candidate—even if true—is considered a smear."

Just what is a ghost writer? How extensively are they used?

A ghost writer is simply a professional wordsmith who writes speeches for people in public life. Although most public figures are reluctant to admit it, most do not write their own speeches. They usually generate the subject matter and ideas for the speech and then turn it over to the ghost to research the material to be used and put it together in deliverable language.

Since most politicians aren't really funny, where do they get the one-liners and other humor material used in their speeches?

In many cases, the ghost writer also has the talent to write one-liners and light humor into a speech. In other cases, professional humorists or gag writers are used. For instance, in nearly every presidential campaign in the past twenty years, the candidates have had available the services of top-flight humor writers to lighten up their speeches.

One of the busiest men in the business is Robert Orben, former writer for *The Red Skelton Show*, who provides humor material for public speakers ranging from politicians to business executives. In the 1964 presidential campaign, Orben wrote the bulk of the one-liners used by GOP presidential candidate Barry Goldwater. He has since provided similar material to a wide range of people in public life, including Vice-President Spiro Agnew and members of Congress.

CHAPTER 6

What laws govern politics?

Who said, "Ignorance of the law excuses no man; not that all men know the law, but because 'tis an excuse every man will plead, and no man can tell how to refute him"?

John Selden, who lived in England from 1584 to 1654, said it.

What laws govern elections and campaigns?

Two bodies of law primarily—federal and state. There also are municipal and other political subdivision ordinances and regulations which apply.

The most significant legislation in recent years was the Federal Election Campaign Act of 1971, passed by the Senate on December 14, 1971, and by the House on January 19, 1972. Also known as the Campaign Reform Bill, it applies to candidates for federal office only. Included are the president, vice-president, U.S. senators and representatives, delegates and resident commissioners (as in the case of Puerto Rico) to Congress.

In addition, each state specifies certain regulations relating to elections, campaigns, and candidates for both federal and nonfederal offices, as directed by the individual legislatures. For this reason, there is little uniformity.

112

What areas need regulation in political campaigns?

The four major election reform plans advanced in the Ninety-second Congress pretty well covered the waterfront.

The general areas they identified included political broadcasts, equal time provisions, disclosures of contributions, and spending limitations. Among some highly thought-of ideas considered but not adopted were the creation of an independent federal agency to oversee the regulation of election practices, and reduction of postal rates for campaign literature.

Essential to the success of any reform, however, is a practical system of enforcement. Heretofore it has been manifestly absent, making the law virtually a mockery.

What was the public's attitude on campaign reform and ceilings on campaign spending?

Highly favorable. According to Dr. Gallup, up to 78 percent of the American people approved.

What does the new Federal Election Campaign Act do? What areas does it cover?

The new law tightens up on political campaign spending in a number of ways. The four main provisions are as follows:

1. It sets a ceiling on the amount candidates for federal office may spend for media.

2. It stiffens reporting requirements associated with campaigns, including more frequent reports, and detailed lists of contributors and amounts donated.

3. It sets limits on how much candidates and their families may contribute to their own campaigns.

4. Extensive record-keeping requirements are established relating to the receipt of funds donated to political committees supporting candidates.

How does the media spending limit work? Is there a precise formula?

The candidate has a choice between a formula or an overall ceiling on how much he spends for the communications media in his campaign.

The basic formula is that he may spend $.10 for every potential voter, age eighteen or over, or he may merely use $50,000 as his upper limit. The choice is up to him, and he may use whichever amount is greater.

In House races, virtually all candidates will resort to the $50,000 ceiling as their limit since few, if any, House districts contain sufficient people, let alone potential voters, to equal or exceed the $50,000 limit. The determination of the total number of eligible voters will be made by the U.S. Census Bureau on an annual basis for both congressional districts and states.

Candidates for president, vice-president, and the Senate will, in most cases, use the $.10-per-voter formula, with the presidential and vice-presidential candidates lumped together as one race since they are not separated on the ballot.

The bill also provides for an "escalator" in the ceiling in the event that the cost of living rises. In accordance with that provision, the $50,000 limit was adjusted upwards to $52,150 for the 1972 campaign on the basis of certification by the secretary of labor to the comptroller general that the U.S. city average All-items Consumer Price Index had increased 4.3 percent from its 1970 annual average.

What were the spending limits for congressional campaigns before passage of the 1971 Campaign Reform Act? How about presidential campaigns?

The amounts were limited to the lesser of either:

1. The amount set in state law for the specified office, *or*

2. In the case of a Senate candidate, a maximum of $10,000 or an amount obtained by multiplying 3 cents by the total votes cast at the last general election in the state for all candidates for U.S. Senator, but not exceeding $25,000.

3. In the case of a House candidate, a maximum of $2,500, or an amount obtained by multiplying 3 cents by the total votes cast at the last general election for all candidates for the House in the congressional district, but not exceeding $5,000.

The previous limit on presidential campaigns was $3 million.

Which communications media are affected by the provisions of the Campaign Reform Act? Did Congress specifically identify them?

Congress did include definitions. The exact wording of the conference report passed by both the House and Senate in reaching a compromise defined communications media as "broadcasting stations, newspapers, magazines, outdoor advertising facilities, and telephones."

With respect to telephones, however, Congress declared that the provisions of the law applied "only if such spending or expenditure is for the costs of telephones, paid telephonists, and automatic telephone equipment, used by a candidate for federal elective office to communicate with potential voters (excluding any costs of telephones incurred by a volunteer for use of telephones by him)."

The definition of broadcasting station also includes community antenna television systems as well as radio and television stations themselves. Direct mail is excluded from the limitation.

Does the media spending limit apply to an entire campaign or does it consider the primary and general election as separate?

The limits apply to each campaign as unrelated to the other. In other words, the slate is wiped clean after the primary. Each primary, general, special, or runoff election is treated as a completely separate entity for reporting purposes as far as the limits are concerned.

To illustrate, let's assume that a House candidate in 1972 underwent a primary, then a runoff following the primary, and then the general election. The maximum he could spend for media thus could total $156,450, based on $52,150 for each of those campaigns.

May the candidate allocate his communications media expenditures in any way he wishes? Could he put it all into television ads?

There is one specific prohibition—the candidate may not spend more than 60 percent of his media budget in broadcasting. Thus, $31,290 of the $52,150 ceiling is all he could put into radio and television advertising.

The breakdown of the remainder is completely at his own discretion.

Are there any special advertising rates for political candidates?

Yes. As part of the Federal Election Campaign Act of 1971, the Congress also amended the Communications Act of 1934 concerning rate schedules for political candidates.

The law states:

The charges made for the use of any broadcasting station by any person who is a legally qualified candidate for any public office in connection with his campaign for nomination for election, or election, to such office shall not exceed—

(1) during the 45 days preceding the date of a primary or primary run-off election and during the sixty days preceding the date of a general or special election in which such person is a candidate, the lowest unit charge of the station for the same class and amount of time for the same period; and

(2) at any other time, the charges made for comparable use of such station by other users thereof.

The law also specifies what the rate schedule must be for newspaper and magazine advertising for candidates for federal offices. Those charges "shall not exceed the charges made for comparable use of such space for other purposes."

Does the Campaign Reform Act limit other campaign spending besides amounts used for the media? I'm thinking about campaign staff hire costs, travel, auditorium rentals, campaign headquarters, and the like.

No. Such a limitation was proposed and debated during consideration of the bill by the House, but it was defeated.

What political committees are covered by the federal campaign law?

Every one which is involved in any way with campaigns for federal elective office if they receive or expect to receive, or spend or expect to spend, more than $1,000 in a calendar year. Thus, the coverage is broadened substantially. Under the previous law, for example, federal reporting requirements did not apply to committees operating in only one state or the District of Columbia.

Are federal employees still prevented from participating in partisan campaigns for elective office?

There are limitations on federal employees becoming involved in political campaigns under the Political Activities Act of 1939, usually called the Hatch Act. It was conceived as a means to protect federal workers from pressure from government officials to support partisan political interests. That law wasn't affected by the 1971 Campaign Reform Act.

Government workers are prevented from engaging in most partisan political activity, including fund-raising, campaign organizing, and soliciting votes. They also may not seek elective office in races where a national political party is involved.

Although a U.S. Court in mid-1972 declared unconstitutional that part of the Hatch Act barring federal employees from participating in politics, a three-judge panel subsequently stayed the new ruling from going into effect pending review of the decision by the U.S. Supreme Court, probably in 1973. Meantime, the Hatch Act remains in effect.

Have there been any cases of federal employees found violating the Hatch Act? If so, what happens to them?

There have been occurrences from time to time. The most recent concerned six high-level General Services Administration officials in Washington, D.C., in early 1972. All were suspended from 30 to 90 days without pay for having solicited money from employees in 1971 to buy tickets for a "Salute to the President" dinner.

The three civil service commissioners, two Republican appointees and one Democrat, authorized the suspensions on the recommendation of a hearing examiner who concluded that the six employees had violated the law.

What is the ceiling on contributions by a candidate or his own family?

A candidate, together with members of his immediate family, may not contribute more than the following combined total from personal funds: House races, $25,000; Senate races, $35,000; and presidential or vice-presidential races, $50,000.

The immediate family definition includes the candidate's "spouse, and any child, parent, grandparent, brother, or sister of the candidate, and the spouses of such persons."

Are contribution limits set on anyone except candidates and their families?

No. The Campaign Reform Bill acknowledged that the previous limitations contained in the Corrupt Practices Act were meaningless because they were easily circumvented.

For example, the previous limitation specified that an individual might contribute no more than $5,000 within a calendar year to a candidate or national committee in connection with any campaign for federal office. However, the law did not prohibit that same individual from donating $5,000 to each of several different committees supporting that same candidate. In addition, that individual's spouse and other members of the family could contribute up to $5,000 each in the same way.

Does the Election Reform Law prevent federal candidates from promising jobs if they win? For example, could I expect to get a promise from a congressional candidate that he would hire me if I joined his campaign and he won?

You well might get the promise, but it would be illegal for him to make it. The law specifically prohibits such promises. The penalty for the candidate is a fine of "not more than $1,000 or imprisonment of not more than one year, or both."

So while you might receive a guarantee of employment if you help a candidate win, you probably never would get it in writing or in the presence of witnesses unless the candidate were ignorant of the provision. Incidentally, it existed in the earlier law as well.

What are the reporting requirements for contributions to federal campaigns? How have they been stiffened?

Reports now are required more frequently and are more detailed as a result of the 1971 Campaign Reform Bill. All contributions in excess of $100 within a calendar year must be reported by the recipient and must include the full name, address, occupation, and business address of the donor.

In an election, a minimum of eight public expense reports is required of every candidate and every political committee which expects to receive or expend more than $1,000 during the calendar year. These reports are in addition to an initial registration report committees must make.

The required reports are due on March 10, June 10, September 10, fifteen days before election day, five days before the election, and a post-election report by January 31 following the election. The fifteen- and five-day reports must be filed before the state primary election dates as well.

Further, any contribution exceeding $5,000 in the last five days before the election day must be reported within forty-eight hours of receipt to the appropriate supervisory officer, either by telegraph or hand-delivered letter.

U.S. Senate candidates must file these reports with the Secretary of the Senate, House candidates with the Clerk of the U.S. House, and presidential candidates with the Comptroller General. Copies also must be forwarded to the secretaries of state at state capitals. In every instance, they will be available for inspection by the press and public upon demand.

Those reporting requirements sound formidable. Is the law going to work?

There is doubt that all of the administrative requirements will be retained, at least in so far as the frequency of reports is concerned.

One problem which has already surfaced is the volume of paper work generated by the legislation. For instance, the Clerk of the House of Representatives estimated receipt of about 9,000 reports five days before the 1972 election, threatening to create serious problems in processing and making them public within the required forty-eight hours.

Can you single out any specific instances of technical violations of the federal election law as it existed prior to 1972 which were not penalized?

Yes. A review of the filings required by law with the Clerk of the House and the Secretary of the Senate in 1968 and 1970 provides a good example. After the conclusion of the 1968 campaign, 107 candidates failed to submit the required reports. In 1970, some twenty-five did not comply.

In none of these cases was any action taken against any of the individuals involved. In fact, no action ever has been taken for such violations against any candidate since the Federal Corrupt Practices Act was passed in 1925.

However, a lawsuit was filed on February 9, 1972, against several federal officers charging failure to enforce the law. The action was taken by consumer advocate Ralph Nader and his Public Citizen, Inc., group. The complaint levied charges against the Attorney General, the Clerk of the House, the Secretary of the Senate, and their predecessors. The suit contended that the individuals named "caused and encouraged wholesale, widespread and flagrant violation" of the 47-year-old law governing campaign financing and "fostered corruption, fraud and dishonesty in the electoral process."

The court suit, interestingly, came one day after President Nixon signed the new Federal Elections Campaign Act which was to become effective sixty days later on April 7, 1972. The filing was generally considered to be a challenge aimed at assuring future enforcement of provisions of the new legislation which repealed the Corrupt Practices Act.

How did the Federal Corrupt Practices Act of 1925 come about?

The bill was introduced to amend the then-existing postal law to reclassify the salaries of postal workers and increase postal rates. What ultimately became the provisions of the act was added in the Senate Committee on Post Offices and Post Roads report on the House bill. The new title came about as a result of the Senate Committee action.

Many of the provisions of the 1925 act had been included in an earlier Federal Corrupt Practices Act, passed in 1910. That legislation was essentially a reporting statute for political committees operating in two or more states and primarily relating to House elections. The 1910 act, as passed initially, did not set ceilings on congressional campaign expenditures. Those limitations were added in 1911 in the form of an amendment.

Interestingly, the 1910 act was subjected to a court test and found unconstitutional by the U.S. Supreme Court in *Newberry v. U.S.* in 1921. The court held that the power of Congress to regulate elections for federal office did not extend to the primary or nominating process but was limited only to general elections. However, a 1941 Supreme Court ruling in the case of *U.S. v. Classic* in effect overruled the *Newberry* decision. In the 1941 case, the Court held that Congress does have the constitutional power to regulate primary elections where they are an integral part of the election to the U.S. Senate or House.

Are campaign contributions now deductible on federal income tax returns?

Yes. As a result of an amendment to the Revenue Act of 1971, credit may be taken for contributions made to candidates in federal, state, or local elections or to a political committee.

The ceiling is $50 for a single taxpayer or $100 for a married couple filing a joint return. The figure can be deducted either from the individual's taxable income or half of it may be subtracted from the total tax bill as a tax credit up to a maximum of $12.50 for a single person and $25 for a married couple filing a joint return. The impact of the saving will be determined by the amount of the taxpayer's contribution and the tax bracket he is in.

One caution: the $50 deduction (or $100 for a couple) can be used only once in a calendar year. In short, you can't contribute that amount to several different candidates and deduct it all.

What about contributions of property or services? Can an individual get credit on his tax return for those?

No. Cash contributions are the only kind of assistance for which a taxpayer may claim credit on his return.

The Revenue Act of 1971, which provided for the tax credits and deductions, specifically defined what is eligible. The law reads: "The term 'political contribution' means a contribution or gift of money. . . ." The Campaign Reform law also included wording on the contribution of volunteers' time. The definition carefully qualifies where the services of volunteers stand. It says "the word [contribution] shall not be construed to include services provided without compensation by individuals volunteering a portion or all of their time on behalf of a candidate or a political committee."

What's the status of the proposal to allow taxpayers to "check off" funds for presidential candidates directly on their income tax returns?

That plan was passed by the Congress as part of the Revenue Act of 1971, to go into effect in 1972. It permits the taxpayer to indicate on his federal income tax return whether he wishes to have $1.00 of his taxes earmarked for presidential campaign purposes ($2.00 in the case of married couples) and to which political party or to a nonpartisan general presidential campaign fund.

What happens if the taxpayer fails to check his intention of contributing to the presidential campaign fund?

Nothing. Funds from that individual's tax payment will not be used for this purpose.

What are the mechanics of the plan? How much will the parties get?

The law specifies a precise formula for the allocation of the presidential campaign moneys.

Major-party candidates would be entitled to public financing in an amount equal to $.15 multiplied by the number of U.S. residents eighteen or older as of the first day of June of the presidential election year. The term "major party" is defined in the law as one which received at least 25 percent of the total vote cast in the immediately preceding presidential contest.

Minor-party candidates would be funded under a more complicated formula. Their vote in the immediately preceding presidential election would be divided into the average of the votes received by the major parties. The average major party allocation then would be multiplied by the minor party percentage to provide the amount to be received.

For example, if a minor party received five million votes in the immediately preceding presidential election, and the two major parties polled a total of sixty million votes, the equation would be thirty million divided by five million, or one-sixth the amount each major party is eligible to receive.

In this instance, minor party is defined as one which received more than 5 percent but less than 25 percent of the popular vote cast in the preceding election.

What about minor parties which received less than 5 percent of the vote in the preceding presidential contest? Would they have an entitlement?

Yes. Under the law, they are considered "new" parties and can share in the public financing after the election, if they obtain more than 5 percent of the vote. The percentage would be determined as outlined above but it would be based on the current rather than preceding election statistics. A party garnering less than 5 percent of the vote would receive no funds.

When would the parties receive the funding?

First, they must decide whether they want it. That decision brings with it acceptance of a limitation that they cannot spend more on the general campaign than the entitlement of $.15 times the number of persons eighteen or older in the United States. In addition, the parties may not accept contributions for the general campaign if sufficient money is in the public fund to pay the full entitlement. Only if there is not enough money in that account may the parties then accept contributions and only in an amount to make up the deficit.

The timing of the payments will depend upon completion of certification of the candidates by the Comptroller General during the presidential election. Up until then, the money simply accumulates, in effect, until it is disbursed.

Just how significant is the tax checkoff in terms of dollars? What would have been provided in the 1972 presidential elections if the procedure had gone into effect for calendar year 1972?

The numbers speak for themselves. If the checkoff had been in effect when taxpayers filed their returns by the April 15 deadline in 1972, an estimated $20.4 million would have been paid into the campaign treasuries of each of the two major party candidates. If Alabama Governor George C. Wallace had been on the ballot as a third-party candidate, he would have received approximately $6.3 million.

Obviously, the dollars involved are significant.

What happens if there isn't enough money in each party's fund to meet the entitlement?

What you're talking about is the situation where not enough people check off a dollar for a particular party. In that event, the funds from the nonpartisan general presidential campaign fund would be allocated on the basis of a formula. The general campaign fund would be financed from the tax returns of those who wish to support the public campaign fund but do not express a party preference.

If the general fund isn't able to meet a particular party's entitlement, then it can accept contributions from individuals, but only up to the amount of the entitlement.

All of this seems complicated. Will it work?

It remains to be seen. However, the public funding concept does eliminate the enormous strain on political parties involved in raising money for a presidential campaign.

Why was the tax checkoff so bitterly debated in Congress? What were the arguments pro and con?

The Democrats contended the system would broaden the base of campaign financing. Senator John O. Pastore (D–R.I.), the sponsor of the key amendment establishing the checkoff system, which passed in 1971, said the new procedure provided "an opportunity for the ordinary citizen to work his will in an area that all too often has been the special province of the large contributor or the vested interest."

Senator Robert Dole (R–Kan.), wasn't buying that thesis. The Republican National Committee chairman called the Pastore plan "a blatant partisan attempt to fund the Democratic opposition to President Nixon in 1972." The bill was later amended to go into effect after the 1972 elections.

Is the concept of providing federal funds for presidential campaigns new?

Actually, no. President Theodore Roosevelt first proposed it nearly sixty years ago.

The plan didn't reach the legislative stage until 1966, however, when

Congress passed a bill to provide equal amounts to the two major parties with a share to minority parties polling more than five million votes in the preceding presidential election. However, that plan gave taxpayers only the choice of earmarking $1.00 for a general presidential campaign fund or not doing so at all. There was no provision, as is now on the books, for the allocation to a specific party.

Largely because of partisan battling, no progress on the so-called tax checkoff came until 1971. And even with the enactment of that legislation, it is not absolutely certain that it will not be revoked before the 1976 presidential election.

How did the original 1966 Presidential Election Campaign Fund work?

Taxpayers, in filing their tax returns in 1968 (for calendar 1967), would have had the option of authorizing $1.00 from their tax returns ($2.00 in the case of married couples) for assignment to the Presidential Election Campaign Fund.

The legislation provided for the General Accounting Office to reimburse the political parties for actual presidential campaign expenses incurred after September 1 of a presidential election year. The funds were to have been made available to major parties, defined as those receiving fifteen million votes or more in the immediately preceding presidential election. Each party thus qualifying would have received equal amounts under this formula: $1.00 for each vote cast for president in the preceding election minus five million votes for each party. Had the plan been implemented as proposed for the 1968 election, some $60 million would have been divided equally between the Republicans and the Democrats on the basis of seventy million voters in 1964. Subtracting the five million for each party left sixty million times $1.00, or $30 million for each party. Minor parties would have been entitled to receive $1.00 for every vote they received above five million in the immediately preceding election.

What happened? Why didn't the law go into effect?

Technically, it did go into effect since it was passed by both houses of Congress and signed by the president in 1966. However, early in 1967, an ultimately successful movement began in the Senate to repeal the law. After a number of votes on amendments, making the issue the lengthiest Senate debate of 1967, the campaign fund plan was shelved until guidelines for its operation could be written. They never were, but new legislation was.

Is it definite that the money from the tax checkoff will make it to the campaign coffers of presidential candidates?

No. The final legislative action taken on the Revenue Act of 1971, which included the checkoff, was the enactment of a compromise version of the bill which emerged from the Senate–House Conference Committee.

That compromise required that Congress take appropriations action which would actually place the moneys in the fund. In other words, although the taxpayers indicate where they want their dollar to go for the 1976 presidential campaign, Congress must still act before the funds reach the destination. Assuming that the House and Senate do not balk at making the appropriation, there is the further possibility of a presidential veto.

Thus, while the law is on the books specifying a mechanism for funding presidential campaigns, possible roadblocks exist.

What does "equal time" mean in so far as political campaigns are concerned?

The equal time provision requires radio and television stations to treat all candidates for the same office alike.

If a station provides free time to a candidate for public office, each competing candidate can request equal time. The same holds true in the sale of advertising time or a combination of free and paid time.

The governing statute is the Federal Communications Act of 1934, as amended, and the rules of the Federal Communications Commission.

Does this mean that the time of day and the day of the week must be identical?

No. The station is not required to provide exactly the same time periods. The key guideline is that the times be comparable in desirability.

For example, if candidate A were given fifteen minutes at 7 P.M., which is prime time, and candidate B received the same amount of time at midnight, there clearly would be discrimination on the part of the station in behalf of candidate A.

What if a candidate buys or tries to buy a far larger amount of advertising time than his opponent, say in a senatorial race? Can a station refuse to sell the time because of the imbalance? Does it have to give the other candidate free time to compensate?

Neither of the above applies. The only limit to the purchase of time is as spelled out in the Campaign Reform Act which limits media spending in federal campaigns. Stations are not obliged to do other than make available comparable time for purchase.

What if a station makes an offer of free time to candidates in an election, and one of them refuses it? Does that prevent the others from availing themselves of the time?

No. But the one who refused could later seek equal time. Whether the station granted time later would depend on such factors as the timing of the request, previous schedule commitments, and so forth.

How about the weekly reports that many congressmen air on radio? Do the stations using these tapes have to provide a similar amount of time?

Yes, once the incumbent congressman has become a candidate for reelection, which usually is the point at which he announces his intention to run again. That point marks the start of his campaign.

It should be noted that many stations, and the incumbents themselves, automatically terminate the weekly report type of program once an announcement of candidacy is made.

Does the equal time provision apply to radio and television news broadcasts? In other words, does the station have to give opposing candidates exactly the same coverage?

No. Bona fide news is outside the purview of the equal time requirements. The stations have the responsibility and prerogative of using their best judgment as to what qualifies as news. Press conferences, news interviews, documentaries, and on-the-spot coverage of events ordinarily fall into the category of news.

Is the equal time requirement working properly?

There is considerable debate on this point. One major network executive, Columbia Broadcasting System President Frank Stanton, told the Senate Commerce Committee on March 3, 1971, that because the law "requires equal time for every candidate for an office, however insignificant or frivolous his candidacy, the practical effect of the law has been to deny free broadcast time to major candidates or to force free time to be shared with fringe candidates."

However, Congressman John B. Anderson (R–Ill.), speaking on the floor on November 29, viewed the matter differently. "In 1964, there were twenty states where there were only two candidates running as candidates of major parties . . . no minority party candidates or so-called frivolous fringe candidates," he said. "Yet . . . only 27 percent of the television stations offered any free time at all to the major party candidates."

Strong opposition to repealing the equal time provision was evident in House debate in November 1971, with many congressmen adamant against lessening the specificity of the existing law. Discussion of the issue is certain to continue in what at times can be fairly called a controversy.

What recourse does a candidate have if he feels that he has not been treated equitably by a radio or television station?

The Federal Communications Commission is empowered to adjudicate such matters.

However, the FCC, as a rule, urges that such disputes be ironed out between the parties wherever possible. When a candidate feels he has no other avenue, he should file a complaint with the FCC, with a complete listing of all of the facts bearing on the case. The filing should be made as quickly as possible with a copy to the station concerned. Each party should have a copy of every communication the other addresses to the FCC on the matter, and the FCC should have a copy of all exchanges between the two parties.

What is the so-called "fairness doctrine"? Is that the same as equal time?

The "fairness doctrine" is broader than just the equal time requirements which relate to political broadcasts. The doctrine is the obligation of broadcasters to afford reasonable opportunity for the presentation of opposing views when controversial issues of public importance are broadcast.

The instances of its application have been growing during the last several years as more and more stations have begun airing editorials. For instance, a station might urge reductions in the level of military spending and state the reasons for its position. A local organization, such as a post of the American Legion, might disagree and ask to present its arguments. The station doubtless would provide the time for the rebuttal.

What happened to the idea of televising debates between presidential candidates?

The equal time provision is tagged as the culprit.

If time were provided for presidential candidates to debate or appear individually, then all contenders would be entitled to equal amounts of time, including minor party candidates and all of the so-called fringe candidates.

In 1960, however, the nation was able to see the historic debates between Richard M. Nixon and John F. Kennedy. They came about only because Congress repealed the equal time provision of the law for that election. Thus, the networks were able legally to provide the time for the candidates of the two major parties to meet face to face without having to provide similar time to all other candidates.

What are the laws governing conflict of interest of public officials?

A number of procedures are in effect relating to financial disclosure to thwart conflicts of interest.

In Congress, both the Senate and the House have requirements for limited annual disclosure of certain financial interests. In the Senate, it is confined to honoraria of $300 or more, personal political contributions received by the senator including the source, and any gift of more than $50 from nonrelatives. The House report is a two-part filing, one part of which is public and the other confidential, to be opened only if a majority of the Standards of Official Conduct Committee votes to do so. The public portion must list any interest or position held by the filer in "any business entity doing a substantial business with the federal government or subject to federal regulatory agencies in which the ownership is in excess of $5,000 fair market value as of the date of filing or from which income of $1,000 or more was derived during the preceding calendar year." The confidential section of the report must contain a detailed amplification and identification of the listings of the first part.

In the executive branch, a 1965 executive order requires cabinet members and White House staff to complete confidential conflicts of interest forms, which are reviewed by a presidential aide for any apparent conflicts.

Federal judges, except for the Supreme Court, must report any outside income every three months to a panel of judges.

Almost four hundred different ethics proposals have been introduced in the Congress. Those favoring more stringent disclosure requirements generally have urged standards that regulate the use of contributions by candidates for personal reasons, defining when political contributions should be considered tax-free gifts and when they should come under tax laws, better definition of what constitutes a political expenditure, and a workable definition of conflict of interest itself.

Both the House and Senate have established select committees to oversee the ethics of members of those bodies. In the case of the House, a code of ethics was adopted as well as the requirement for an annual financial disclosure report by members of Congress, their principal assistants, and professional members of committee staffs.

The code of ethics specifies, among other things, that members, officers, and employees of the House:

1. Receive no compensation nor permit any to accrue to their beneficial interest, the receipt of which would occur by virtue of influence improperly exerted from their positions in the Congress.

2. Accept no gifts of substantial value from any person, organization, or corporation having a direct interest in legislation before the Congress.

3. Accept no honorarium for a speech, writing for publication, or other similar activity, from any person, organization, or corporation in excess of the usual and customary value for such services.

4. Keep campaign funds separate from personal funds. No campaign funds shall be converted to personal use in excess of reimbursement for legitimate and verifiable prior campaign expenditures.

5. Treat as campaign contributions all proceeds from testimonial or other fund-raising events if the sponsors of such affairs do not give clear notice in advance to the donors or participants that the proceeds are intended for other purposes.

6. Retain no one from their clerk-hire allowance who does not perform duties commensurate with the compensation he receives.

Are the safeguards working?

Not entirely, and it is doubtful that an all-encompassing, enforceable set of regulations ever will be put on the books. In the *Job of the Congressman*, by Rep. Morris K. Udall (D–Ariz.) and Donald G. Tacheron, the problem is discussed:

"Existing rules and statutes dealing with the problem are imprecise and difficult to apply to particular situations faced by individual members. Moreover, little uniformity of congressional practice exists in the handling

Election bets have been with us since the beginning of political campaigns, as indicated by this offer to wager on the 1876 presidential election. Courts have held that such bets are against public policy and have declared them void and uncollectable, yet betting on the outcome of elections continues. *From the Collection of the Hayes Memorial Library, Fremont, Ohio.*

of outside business interests. Accordingly, in a large area of ambiguity the member and his conscience must make the decisions."

Are election bets legal?

Yes and no. Courts have held that such bets are against public policy on the grounds that they could corrupt the election, and have therefore declared them void and uncollectable. At the same time, millions of dollars change hands every election, and Las Vegas gamblers even list the odds on the outcome of a presidential contest. Outside of Nevada, however, winners of bets of this kind could find them uncollectable if the case got into the courts.

PART 3

Politics: Checks and Balances

CHAPTER 7

What makes Congress work?

Who are members of Congress supposed to represent—their constituencies or the national interest?

As a practical matter, both.

Two concepts evolved in England in the seventeenth and eighteenth centuries concerning the role of the legislator. One was the delegation theory. It held that a member of Parliament was obliged to respond to the views of his constituency, rather than his own. The other was that of virtual representation, which saw the officeholder as free to use his own judgment since he was a caretaker of the country as a whole.

In colonial America, the tendency was to oppose the virtual representation approach. However, what we have today is probably closer to that concept. In *O Congress*, Congressman Donald Riegle (R–Mich.) recounts a conversation he had with Senate Minority Leader Hugh Scott (R–Pa.) in 1971:

"Then, Scott delivered some heartfelt remarks about what a Congressman really should be. He said a Congressman has to be independent and make his own best judgments. 'His job,' Scott added, 'is not to weigh the mail but to weigh the evidence.' He stressed the personal agonies such judgments often impose on decent and reasonable men. He said good people can and do come out on different sides of the same issue."

In practice, the question of state or district versus national interest can come into conflict. For instance, although a congressman may be intellectually committed to free trade, he may well vote against legislation lowering or eliminating certain tariff barriers because such action would adversely affect an industry in his district. The flood of low-cost imports into the country competing with the products of his district could cause widespread unemployment there.

In such an instance, the congressman has little choice. He might well try to amend the bill to include a relief provision for the affected industry in his district, through a federal grant of some kind or a retraining program for workers displaced by the foreign competition. Failing that, he most likely would vote against the legislation.

Edmund Burke, the British statesman, summed up the issue in a speech to his constituents on November 3, 1774, on the occasion of his election to Parliament. Said Burke:

> Certainly, gentlemen, it ought to be the happiness and glory of a representative to live in the strictest union, the closest correspondence, and the most unreserved communication with his constituents. Their wishes ought to have great weight with him; their opinions high respect; their business unremitted attention. It is his duty to sacrifice his repose, his pleasure, his satisfactions to theirs, and above all, ever, and in all cases, to prefer their interests to his own.
>
> But his unbiased opinion, his mature judgment, his enlightened conscience, he ought not to sacrifice to you, to any man, or to any set of men living. These he does not derive from your pleasure—no, nor from the law and the constitution. They are a trust from providence for the abuse of which he is deeply answerable. Your representative owes you not his industry only but his judgment, and he betrays instead of serving you if he sacrifices it to your opinion.

What are the requirements to be a senator or a member of the House of Representatives?

A senator must be at least thirty years old, a citizen of the United States for at least nine years, and a resident of the state he represents.

A representative must be twenty-five, a citizen for at least seven years, and reside in the state from which he seeks election.

Can I run for the U.S. House even though I am not a resident of the congressional district I am seeking to represent?

Yes. The Constitution merely specifies that you must be a resident of the state in which the district is located. Practically speaking, however, it makes sense to reside in the district, thereby eliminating the charge by potential opponents that you are a carpetbagger.

Briefly, what are the arguments for and against extending the present two-year term in the U.S. House of Representatives to four years, as has been proposed from time to time?

The argument favoring four-year terms for House members centers on the contention that two-year terms cause congressmen to spend too much time campaigning. As a practical matter, many never really stop campaigning because the time between elections is so short. The argument for the longer terms propounds the view that elective pressure would be lessened and the congressmen then would have more time to legislate and be less political in their votes.

The counterargument against changing the two-year term holds that House members are more responsive to their constituents because they are on the ballot every other year. Proponents of this view say that the two-year term was deliberate, in contrast to the six-year Senate term, to keep one house of the legislative branch close to the people.

Interestingly, surveys show that although most House members would welcome the longer term, most would also vote against changing the present length.

Is there a specific date for the beginning and end of the terms for congressmen and senators?

Yes. Their terms begin and end at 12 noon on January 3 following the November election. When a member fills a House vacancy at a special election, his term of service begins that day. For senators elected or appointed after adjournment, service begins on the day after election or on the date of appointment. With the Senate in session, their terms begin when they take the oath of office.

Does the title "congressman" apply to members of both the House and Senate?

Technically yes, since they are all members of Congress.

But in practice, the term applies only to members of the House, who are generally addressed with the title of congressman. A senator will never refer to himself as a congressman but will call himself a member of Congress on occasion. Current usage is senator. House members are almost never addressed as representative in using the spoken word. While sometimes seen in letter salutations, it is not a common form.

What are the average ages for the House and Senate? Who are the oldest and youngest members of Congress?

At the beginning of the Ninety-second Congress, the average age of the entire Congress was 52.7 years. Senators averaged somewhat higher than House members with 56.4 versus 51.9 years.

The oldest member in the Ninety-second Congress was Rep. Emanuel Celler, a New York Democrat who was 84 when he was defeated for renomination in 1972. The youngest member of Congress was Georgia Democrat Dawson Mathis, thirty-one in 1972.

In the Senate in 1972, Vermont Republican George Aiken was the oldest at eighty, and California Democrat John Tunney the youngest at thirty-eight. Aiken gained the title of oldest Senator upon the death in 1972 of eighty-one-year-old Allen Ellender of Louisiana.

Is a legal background necessary for service in the Senate and House?

It's helpful but not necessary. In the Ninety-second Congress, 236 of the 435 House members were lawyers, as were sixty-five of the one hundred senators. This amounted to 54 percent in the House and 65 percent in the Senate.

The remaining members had varied backgrounds and experience ranging from business to journalism to medicine to teaching and other professions.

When I've got a beef about something, somebody usually suggests I write my congressman. Does it do any good?

The safest answer is that it won't hurt.

While the impact of a single letter is generally not significant, it could be under certain circumstances. You might be the only constituent to point out a problem that sorely needs correcting. If the congressman or senator investigates and determines that you were right, he well might introduce legislation to effect the necessary change or ask the appropriate agency of government to revise its procedures, depending on whether the case involved a legislative or executive matter.

Another reason to write is simply to let your congressman or senator know what your views are. If a thousand constituents wrote on the same issue, the congressman definitely would take notice. Further, he might not have been aware that there was any strong feeling on the matter one way or the other and might have been undecided himself. So you can help him represent his district by telling him where you stand.

If you contact him about a problem involving you and the government, he will look into it and get an answer for you. A good part of every congressional office's time is devoted to what is called casework. It includes constituent problems with the armed services, Social Security, Medicare, veterans benefits, and so on. When a congressman makes such an inquiry, he is usually able to get a prompter and perhaps even more favorable answer, without the red tape that the ordinary citizen might encounter.

One further comment is in order. Don't harangue your congressman when you write, even if you disagree with him. The best approach is the rational one. Detail your views as precisely and dispassionately as you can. A well-thought-out, reasonable letter makes a far better impact.

I've heard it said that most members of Congress never read their incoming mail and some don't even sign their own letters. Is this true?

Yes, particularly in cases where they receive a large volume of mail on the same subject. What happens is that the congressman determines his position, and his staff will use that information either for individually typed letters or those done on automatic typewriters.

Although the practice varies from office to office, most House members at least see outgoing letters to constituents even though they may not sign them all personally. In the Senate, the mail volume frequently is so large that it would be physically impossible for a busy senator from a large state to read and sign every piece of correspondence.

Personalities come into play, however, and some congressmen are adamant about nothing going out the door without their knowing about it. Others have such great confidence in their chief assistants that they are less concerned.

Signature machines are widely used in the Senate but only on a limited basis in the House. In the latter, it is more common to have staff members sign the congressman's name to correspondence. In such cases, while members may read and personally approve every reply going out, they will sign only a comparative handful to save time.

How many letters does the average Senate office receive every day? An average House office?

Since the size of each state varies considerably, the flow of mail into Senate offices also varies. But each senator can expect to receive from one hundred up to one thousand communications daily. These totals will jump substantially at the height of a burning national issue when thousands of letters will pour in each day.

In the House, the mail into a congressman's office averages between fifty and one hundred letters each day. In addition, most Senate and House members have state and district offices which relay local calls from constituents.

Congressmen have free mailing privilege. What can they use this for? What are the regulations?

The franking privilege, as it is called, is the free mail benefit provided to members of Congress. The basic ground rule is that it may be used only for official business.

If a member were to send out checks for payment of his personal household and nonoffice bills under the frank, he would be violating the privilege. In addition to official correspondence, he is permitted to use the frank on his newsletters providing they deal with subjects relating to his job, *Congressional Record* excerpts, government publications, and similar material. However, the privilege applies only to surface mail. Any faster form, air mail or special delivery, requires the use of stamps as it does for any other citizen.

Prior to the Ninety-first Congress, the Post Office Department exercised limited oversight over the use of the frank, but this has been abandoned. The adjudication now is solely a matter for the Congress itself to determine.

What's the story on Congress' two sessions? Please explain.

Each Congress is composed of two one-year sessions, the first and the second. And the Congresses themselves are numbered consecutively. It is basically a legalism which really doesn't mean much to anyone not on Capitol Hill.

There can be significance which is not immediately apparent, however. For instance, if your senator or congressman introduces a bill late in the second session of a Congress, it is unlikely that the measure will stand much chance of obtaining a hearing, let alone enactment. All legislation not passed by the end of the second session of any Congress automatically dies and must be reintroduced in the following Congress to be eligible for consideration again.

What are the stages that a bill must go through before becoming a law?

First, it must be introduced. Only a member of Congress can file a bill.

Next, it must be scheduled for hearings by the committee to which it has been referred. Then the committee must report it to the floor for vote by the entire body. After this, it goes to the other house for the same sequence of events.

If there are differences, as there frequently are, in the versions enacted by the two bodies, a conference committee is appointed comprising congressmen and senators from the committees of jurisdiction on the bill. This committee meets to try to resolve outstanding differences, usually resulting in a compromise which they feel will be acceptable to each house. The result is then reported back to both bodies in the form of a conference report and voted on again. If it passes, it then goes to the president, who has the option of signing or vetoing it.

The Congress can, and sometimes does, override the veto, but a two-thirds majority in both houses is required. If that majority is not attainable, the measure goes back to committee again to try to develop a bill that will be acceptable to both the Congress and the president.

What's the difference between a bill and an act? What's meant by a public law? What does it mean when a bill has been "pigeonholed"?

Technically, a bill becomes an act after it has been passed by one house. But in popular usage, proposed legislation becomes an act once it is signed into law by the president.

The term "public law" is used to differentiate between a bill dealing with classes of citizens as distinct from a bill which is for the benefit of individuals. Sometimes the difference is not obvious, and a bill for individuals can be classed as a public law because it contains provisions of general legislation.

When a bill has been pigeonholed, it means it has been stalled somewhere along the legislative line. It could be in the committee to which it was referred after introduction, by the House Rules Committee, or in the Senate committee after enactment by the House. There are procedural devices available to help pry legislation out of such pigeonholes, but they are used infrequently.

If only a member of Congress can introduce a bill, how do administration bills get introduced?

Usually, the ranking member of the president's party on the committee of jurisdiction will file the legislation. If the president is a Republican and the Democrats control the Congress, then the introducer will be the highest ranking Republican on the appropriate committee. If the same party controls the White House and the Congress, then the committee chairman will ordinarily put his name on the measure and introduce it.

What's meant by standing committees of the Congress? What are select and joint committees?

"Standing" is a synonym for permanent—that is, standing committees continue in existence from one Congress to the next. At the present time, there are thirty-seven standing committees—twenty-one in the House and sixteen in the Senate.

· Select committees have a limited life-span. They are constituted for a specific purpose and period. Once its reason for existence has been completed, the select committee automatically expires.

A joint committee is one which includes both Senate and House members.

How about subcommittees?

They are a further breakdown within a standing committee charged with specific areas of responsibility. In effect, they undertake special activities in behalf of the full committee. Their findings or decisions are reported to the full committee which then decides on what disposition is to be made of the results.

How much behind-the-scenes work goes into getting a bill enacted into law? How much of legislation is a compromise? How much horse trading is there?

Legislation runs the gamut from noncontroversial to a battle royal. More often than not, the final product passed and signed into law by the president has been altered substantially along the way.

The major work is done in the committees, and the committee chairman is the key man. While he can be overridden by votes within committee, he possesses a great deal of power in merely determining what shall and shall not be considered. The form of the bill as considered on the floor is worked out in committee and is usually what is finally enacted into law. The chairmen, all veterans of floor battles, are careful not to bring out legislation that does not stand a chance of passage. This means that provisions certain to engender strong opposition on the floor may well be modified or eliminated before the bill is reported out of committee.

Another consideration, particularly in the House, is the rule under which the bill comes before the full body. In some cases, as in tax bills, amendments are not permitted. Thus, a congressman can vote only for or against the bill.

The greatest horse trading occurs in the conference committees, when members of the House and Senate attempt to rectify differences in the two bodies' versions of a bill. In *The Congressman*, Charles L. Clapp quotes an unidentified House member as saying about his experience in a conference committee meeting:

"I once sat on a conference committee dealing with a public works bill. The Senate conferees always took a strong position on projects in their states. If a project was outside the states of the conferees, compromise was in order, but they didn't compromise very much on those affecting their own constituencies. I should say some of the House members had the same attitude."

I've heard about the use of discharge petitions to bring bills out of recalcitrant committees. How does this process work? What is a "rider" attached to a bill?

In the House, a bill may be taken out of committee if held longer than thirty days by means of a discharge petition, which requires the signatures of a majority or 218 members when all 435 seats are filled. The bill then is placed on a special calendar, and any of the signers of the petition may call it up on the second or fourth Monday of any month. Twenty minutes' debate is allowed on the motion. If it carries, the House then votes further to consider the bill and then it comes under the general rules.

The procedure is rarely used, generally only on very controversial issues. The most recent example was the so-called "Prayer Amendment" in 1971. A constitutional amendment, it required a two-thirds majority for passage, which it failed to obtain in the House. In fact, a few members who signed the discharge petition voted against it when it came to the floor.

A rider is exactly that—an addition to an appropriations bill that is not necessarily related to the bill and which attempts to "ride" that bill's chances for success. Sometimes a rider will have absolutely no relation to the basic appropriations bill and can even cause its defeat, either on the floor or by presidential veto.

What's a filibuster? Its origin? Does it serve a constructive purpose?

A filibuster is a device used to delay proceedings in a legislative body. Its most familiar use is in the U.S. Senate.

In that body, if one-third of the membership is opposed to cloture, or termination of debate, the filibuster can continue. The House has no parallel. The only delaying tactic commonly used there is the calling of quorums and other limited parliamentary devices which slow down activity but not as effectively as a Senate filibuster.

The word seems to trace back to Dutch, Spanish, and French words meaning pirate, but their point of applicability to the parliamentary scene is indeterminate. The word was in fairly common use in the Congress in the mid-nineteenth century.

Whether the tactic serves a useful purpose can be debated. But the answer frequently given, at least as far as the Senate is concerned, is that it serves to protect the minority and prevents it from being crushed by a majority of less than two-thirds.

What's the origin of the phrase "advise and consent"? What does it mean?

The Constitution uses it as a reference to the powers of the president in relation to the U.S. Senate:

"He shall have power, by and with the advice and consent of the senate, to make treaties, provided two-thirds of the senators present concur; and he shall nominate, and by and *with* the advice and consent of the senate, shall appoint ambassadors, other public ministers and consuls, judges of the supreme court, and all other officers of the United States, whose appointments are not herein otherwise provided for, and which shall be established by law."

The Senate's prerogative has become a source of contention from time to time between it and the White House. President Richard Nixon and the Senate were at odds over Supreme Court appointments particularly, and the Senate defeated two of his nominations which became a national cause célèbre.

Why do some congressmen have poor attendance records? What's more important than being present on the floor, at least when a vote is held?

Not much, really. Among reasons for absence are committee trips away from Washington, appearances before constituent groups, or even a member's own campaign for reelection or for another office.

Not many members of Congress will run the risk of missing too many roll-call votes, however, because such a record makes them vulnerable to campaign attacks by their opponents and criticism from the press.

How effective are lobbyists on legislation? Do they serve a valuable or sinister purpose?

They can be very effective for the cause they serve and valuable to the Congress as well. Their chief function is to provide information regarding a particular point of view. While they are promoting their view, they nevertheless contribute to the study of an issue. In the same sense, constituents themselves, when they organize and send their congressmen and senators petitions, are lobbyists.

The term "lobby" is used in a very broad sense now. Not every group which is so described is required to register as a lobbyist. Lobby groups can influence the course of legislation not only by arguing the pro or con side of a bill but by generating grass roots support to pressure the members.

Where did the term "lobbyist" originate? How much are lobbyists paid?

It first appeared in mid-seventeenth-century England where the reference was "lobbier." Representatives of special interest groups would contact members of the House of Commons in a public room, or lobby, hence the term. The same practice was true in the United States and still is operative in many of the state legislatures which are not as large or complex as the Congress.

The salaries lobbyists receive can range from small retainers to the high professional levels of $50,000 and up.

What kind of weight do labor unions carry with members of Congress? How about business organizations?

Unions carry considerable weight with members whose districts or states are heavily unionized. In some states, their support and endorsement can help to make or break a candidate, especially if they are able to turn out the membership to vote with the union's leadership. Financial support, also a lever available to business groups, likewise is a consideration.

In short, any well-organized group with a large membership, whether it be labor or business, is bound to carry weight with members of Congress.

What's the seniority system which is mentioned so often about Congress? How does it work?

As used in the news media and in books about the national legislature, the seniority system refers to the procedure whereby length of service determines rank on the committees. In other words, the senator or congressman of the majority party who has been on the committee the longest automatically becomes the chairman. In the case of the party in the minority, the most senior member becomes the "ranking," or top, member on the committee of his party. In the same way, chairmanships of the subcommittees generally have been assigned by the chairmen of the committees.

Seniority also is the criterion by which office and parking space for members of Congress is assigned.

Do I understand that each party sets its own seniority rules—that this isn't the action of the entire Congress?

That's right. Each party decides how it will select either committee chairman or ranking minority members, depending on its status as majority or minority party.

Just what is the responsibility of the Committee on Committees? Does each party in Congress have its own Committee on Committees?

Yes. The Committee on Committees is a creation of the two parties in Congress to act on requests of their members for committee assignments. With the 1971 revisions in seniority rules, the committees now have the added responsibility of selecting nominees for chairman and for ranking committee membership. (See Chapter 9.)

In the House and Senate, the majority and minority leaders are the chairmen of their party's Committee on Committees.

What are the arguments for and against the congressional seniority system?

There are many on both sides.

One of the leading proponents of the preservation of the seniority system has been Congressman Emanuel Celler (D–N.Y.), veteran chairman of the House Judiciary Committee, who sums up his attitude in *The Seniority Rule in Congress:*

> Fundamentally, the seniority system avoids the waste implicit in instability of committee composition and management. It invokes the presumption that, other things being equal, the man or woman with the greatest experience in a particular job is best fitted to participate in and lead in its performance. . . . The seniority rule has the added virtue of being objective. It automatically eliminates the intrigues, deals and compromises that characterize election campaigns.

Another Democratic congressman, Richard Bolling of Missouri, said in his book, *Power of the House:* "Of course, seniority does have its beneficial side. It cannot and should not be discarded. One needs experience in being a United States Representative, just as physicians or computer-data analysts do. Knowledge presumably generates competence and special skills."

In his book, *Power in The Senate,* Randall B. Ripley said, "The seniority system acts to protect a person who might be in some danger of being discriminated against for any extraneous reason. This, of course, includes protection of the deviate from the norm of party doctrine, or the majority view among a party. It has protection for the unusual guy."

The House Democratic Study Group put it this way:

> Seniority helps to insulate the Congress from encroachments by the White House and other quarters. At present, a President will not seek dismissal of a committee chairman who does not support his program since such an effort would be futile. However, non-automatic chairmanships would open the door to interference in Congressional affairs by the Chief Executive, especially where he is a member of the majority party. . . . There is no need of outside control over committee chairmen because committee members themselves can spur or veto an unresponsive or obstructionist chairman.

In *The Legislative Process in Congress*, George Galloway noted, "Long service on committees brings members in contact with the personnel of the several departments and helps them to be of service in many little and some big ways to their constituents back home."

A 1945 joint congressional committee which looked into the seniority system declared, "Committee chairmen are sometimes re-elected to Congress because their constituents desire to retain the power and prestige of their office. Long and continued service in Congress would be discouraged by abolition of the seniority system."

On the other side of the question, one of the most persistent critics of the seniority system, particularly when he was a member of Congress, was John Lindsay who later was elected mayor of New York City. Said Lindsay in an essay in *We Propose: A Modern Congress:*

In America's continuing experiment in democracy, the seniority system operates to elevate men to positions of leadership in Congress without regard to any qualification except length of service. As presently practiced, the system is unsound, inflexible, undemocratic, and certainly discouraging to junior Members of Congress. Even the law of the jungle operates on a higher level than the "law" of seniority: the first at least works to assure survival of the fittest; the latter operates only to assure survival of the oldest.

Another disadvantage of using seniority to decide committee leadership positions was made by the House Democratic Study Group which presented arguments on both sides of the issue. Said DSG, "The system denies competent younger men a chance to exercise their leadership talents at the time in life when they are most able to meet the rigors of the job. It is therefore wasteful and inefficient."

George Galloway, writing in *Congress at the Crossroads*, declared:

"One of the greatest drawbacks of the seniority system is that it destroys party responsibility or prevents political parties from performing their campaign promises. For if the chairmen of committees owe their places not to their political parties but to the accident of tenure, then they can follow their own inclinations on legislative matters and disregard the platform pledges and legislative program of the the party leaders."

In *The Seniority System in Congress*, George Goodwin commented:

The seniority system produces a large number of chairmen who are representative of only one element of the party, and that, generally, is a minority element. They represent "stagnant" districts made safe by restrictions on voting, by a one-party monopoly, by the ascendancy of a major interest group, or by an effective rural or urban political machine. Thus, the leaders of Congress, produced by the seniority system, are almost guaranteed to oppose the President, regardless of party, and a new non-constitutional dimension is added to our constitutional system of separation of powers.

Former Congressman Everett G. Burkhalter (D–Calif.) summed up opposition to the seniority system in 1964 when he hold the *Washington Post*:

"These old men have got everything so tied down you can't do anything. I never realized how few people ran things back here. There are 435 members, but about 40 call all the shots and they're nearly all around 70 or 80. They're the committee chairmen and the ranking members. Don't misunderstand me. These men have been damn good Congressmen and served their people and their country well. But it's time for them to get out."

What alternatives are there to the seniority system as presently practiced in the Congress?

A host of ideas has been offered, most of which reflect an increased democratization of the selection process. Some throw out seniority entirely; others reduce its weight in comparison to present usage.

The Democratic Study Group of the House of Representatives proposed these nine possibilities which contain representative samplings of most of the ideas offered:

1. Use the seniority system to nominate chairmen subject to the majority approval by the caucus. This proposal would entail a separate vote in the caucus on the chairman of each committee. If the senior member of a particular committee failed to receive majority approval, the caucus would consider the next most senior member, and so on until a chairman acceptable to the majority was elected.

2. Have the caucus elect committee chairmen from among the three most senior members of each committee. This modification would maintain seniority as the dominant factor in selecting committee chairmen while providing a mechanism for considering the fitness and acceptability of the most senior candidate and possibly bypassing him.

3. Authorize the Speaker to nominate chairmen subject to approval by a majority of the caucus. Should the caucus reject one of the Speaker's

nominations, he would continue making nominations until an acceptable chairman was found.

4. Authorize the majority members of each committee to nominate their chairman subject to caucus approval.

5. Authorize the members of each committee, both majority and minority, to select their own chairman, subject only to approval of the whole House.

6. Establish a new special committee to nominate chairmen subject to majority approval by the caucus. This proposal would retain the present Committee on Committees for consideration of all committee assignments other than the selection of committee chairmen.

7. Set an age limit and require chairmen to give up their chairmanships when they reach that age.

8. Set a limit on the number of years a member can serve as chairman and require that, after serving as chairman, the member leave the committee entirely and begin service on another committee.

9. Rotate the chairmanship among the three top members every two years. Thus, the senior member would be able to serve as chairman only two out of every six years.

Okay, there are a lot of viewpoints. What's the answer?

The answer is that nothing will be done effecting major revisions in the present seniority system. For one thing, it's almost impossible to obtain agreement on the need for abolishing the present system in its entirety. For another, each of the alternatives proposed carries with it the seeds of as many or more problems than the present system has.

In short, there will undoubtedly be continuing efforts made to modify and streamline the present system. But don't look for a major overhaul in the near future.

As one veteran congressman commented, "When I came to Congress as a freshman member years ago, I was all for doing away with the seniority system. But the longer I'm here, the better it looks to me."

What's a "lame-duck" session of Congress? Where did the term come from?

When Congress reconvenes after the November election day, but before the next Congress is sworn in in January, the members who have been defeated are entitled to participate as "lame ducks." Members who have not stood for reelection to the House or Senate, in contrast to members who were defeated, are technically not included in the definition, although the prevailing view is to lump them all together.

Lame-duck Congresses were common prior to 1933 when the Twentieth Amendment to the Constitution was ratified. It changed the start of Congress' annual session from the first Monday in December to January 3 and provided that the terms of senators and representatives end on January 3 instead of March 4. This amendment also provided that the terms of the president and vice-president end on January 20 instead of March 4.

The term has its origin in British stock market jargon and appeared first during the latter half of the eighteenth century. It came to America retaining its original meaning of one who fails to meet his obligations or is unable to meet his engagements. In the English stock market usage, such a person was one who "would waddle out of the alley like a lame duck."

The application to American politics came during the 1860s, although there are some who contend it appeared as early as the 1800s. Today, it is applied broadly to any officeholder whose power is diminished by his imminent departure from office, either as a result of defeat at the polls or a statutory limitation on the length of his term.

Is the Congress a stacked deck in favor of a two-party system? Is there room in the structure for third or fourth parties?

Although it has been some time since a third party existed in the Congress in any size, the system is adaptable to it. George Galloway, in his excellent *History of the House of Representatives*, recounted the third-party question:

> More than five hundred seats in the House have been held over the years by the representatives of minor parties and by a few Independents. During the Thirty-Fourth to Thirty-Seventh Congresses (1855–1863), inclusive, 108 seats were occupied by members of the American Party one of whom, Nathaniel P. Banks of Massachusetts, was chosen Speaker in the Thirty-Fourth Congress. Upwards of forty "Independents" have sat in the House of Representatives in the course of time, among them such memorable figures as George W. Norris of Nebraska and Fiorello La Guardia of New York.

In recent years, there has been only a handful of independents. In the Senate during the Ninety-second Congress, there technically were two, Senators James L. Buckley of New York and Harry F. Byrd, Jr., of Virginia. Buckley listed himself in the *Congressional Directory*, as Conservative–Republican and Byrd as independent. Buckley sat with the Republicans and Byrd with the Democrats and for organizational purposes they were considered as members of those parties. There were no independents in the House in the Ninety-second Congress.

Although all 435 seats in the House of Representatives are up for reelection every two years, how many actually are involved in real contests? How many are ordinarily considered safe for one party or the other?

As a practical matter, although the majority of the House members have opponents, fewer than one hundred districts are considered real battlegrounds by the Republican and Democratic congressional committees. In the remainder, the opposition is frequently *pro forma*, for the sake of having a name on the ballot and not much more. Having even a nominal opponent, however, keeps an incumbent "honest" in that it forces him to mount some sort of campaign to defend his seat.

In *Financing Campaigns in the Public Interest*, a special analysis published by the American Enterprise Institute for Public Policy Research in 1971, Howard R. Penniman had this to say:

> There are genuine contests in no more than 20 to 25 percent of the congressional elections every two years. In 1970, more than 20 percent of the candidates for the House of Representatives were unopposed in the general election. Most of the uncontested seats were in the south, but there were others to be found in Illinois, New York, Massachusetts, and other states normally thought to be competitive. Another and larger group of seats, amounting to more than 40 percent·of the total, were won by such lopsided margins that the winner received a minimum of 65 percent of the votes. Party membership distribution in most of these districts suggests that it is unlikely that serious contests could be mounted in any of them. In fewer than 50 House contests out of a possible 435 in 1970 did the winner hold less than 10 percent margin over his nearest opponent. Even in the 35 senate contests, where the races tended to be closer than for the House, five Senators—four of them in states outside the south—won with more than 65 percent of the vote.

How much turnover is there in the House of Representatives each election?

Between 15 and 20 percent. The average number of seats changing hands between 1940 and 1948 was ninety-six for each new Congress. Between 1950 and 1958, the average dropped to sixty-eight. From 1960 to

1966, it moved up to seventy-two. There were ninety-one new congressmen in 1964, seventy-three in 1966, thirty-nine in 1968, and fifty-six in 1970. The average for the thirty-year period was seventy-five new members per Congress.

What was the greatest turnover in congressional seats?

In 1894, the Republican party made a net gain of 120 seats in the House of Representatives—a record which has since held.

What does a member of Congress owe his party after his election?

He owes his party one thing—his organizational vote. In the House of Representatives, that means casting his ballot for the party's nominee for Speaker of the House and in the Senate for President Pro Tem. After that, unlike the British Parliamentary system with its relatively strict party discipline, each member makes his own decisions, although most tend to follow party patterns.

What's so important about the organizational vote?

It determines which party will control the body—which means control of the chairmanships of the committees, the patronage related thereto, and most importantly, the flow of the legislation. Although that vote, while it is pro forma, may be cast for whomever the member wishes, it is almost always cast for the leader of his own party.

What's the population of the average congressional district?

On the basis of the 1970 census, using a population total of 203,184,-772, the average of the 435 districts is 467,091.

However, the Constitution requires that each state have at least one representative in Congress. Thus, states with populations below the 467,000 figure automatically unbalance the average. Alaska, Wyoming, and Vermont all have fewer people than the average but still have one House member. Three others have populations above that average, Nevada, Delaware, and North Dakota, but will still have only one representative. Compounding the issue further is the case of states like Idaho. With a population of more than 713,000, that state will have two congressmen but their districts will fall below the average figure.

How is the size of a congressional district determined? Does Congress do it or do the states?

The Congress sets the size of the House of Representatives, which is 435 voting members, but the actual apportionment is carried out by the states after the decennial census results are published. Initially, most states elected all of their representatives on an at-large basis. Congress later required that representatives be elected from "districts composed of a contiguous and compact territory." The actual redistricting is always provided by the laws of the states.

What is meant by a "swing" district? A "marginal" district? A "target" district?

A "swing" district refers to one which can go—and has gone—either way: Republican or Democrat.

A "marginal" district is one in which an election is won or lost by no more than five percent of the total vote cast.

"Target" is the designation applied by the opposition party to a district where it hopes to depose an incumbent. Marginal districts are usually always so classified.

Have U.S. senators always been elected by the people?

No. The original provision in the Constitution specified that senators would be elected by the state legislatures.

However, this was changed and direct election by the people effected with ratification of the Seventeenth Amendment to the Constitution. It became effective for senators elected after May 31, 1913.

How is a senator replaced if he dies or resigns before his term ends?

In every case but one, Arizona, the state governor appoints a temporary successor usually within 30 to 60 days after the incumbent's death.

But the voters still have the final say on the appointment, either at the next general election or at a special election, as required by state laws. Since the term of a senator is six years, the winner of that election serves out the remainder of the unexpired term of the previous incumbent.

In Arizona, where the governor does not have the power to appoint a successor, the state law requires that the vacancy be filled at the next general election, provided it comes within six months of the date of the vacancy. Otherwise, the governor must call a special election to fill the seat.

How is a seat filled if a House member dies or resigns before his term expires?

There is no provision for appointments as is the case for most Senate seats. Instead, the state governor must set a date for a special election to fill the vacancy. Most states have laws on the books detailing the time frame within which the governor must act.

How do congressional retirement programs compare with private industry?

If you accept the view that members of Congress are on the same level as executives of large corporations, then they come close. Decide for yourself.

A member of Congress with thirty years of service may retire at age fifty-five, with ten years service at age sixty, and with five years at age sixty-two. For every year of service, he receives a credit of 2.5 percent which is multiplied by the average of his top three years of salary.

Let's assume a 60-year-old senator calls it quits after three terms. That gives him eighteen years times 2.5 percent, or 45 percent. He has at least three years at the $42,500 salary level. His pension therefore is $19,125.

The minimum service time is five years to qualify for the retirement program, and members must contribute 8 percent of their salaries to join it. Other federal service time can be added to the formula, but it is not always equal in value to the congressional time for pension computations. A similar but not identical program is in effect for congressional staff employees who, like members of Congress, are not under federal civil service.

Do members of Congress get any special kind of tax break?

The only tax consideration they are entitled to on their $42,500-a-year salary is a deduction for living expenses, which may not exceed $3,000 within each taxable year. This stems from the fact that many members maintain two residences, one in Washington and one in their home state.

Does a member of Congress pay his staff out of his own pocket?

No, he has an allowance for this purpose made available by the Congress. For a member of the House, the total available for hiring staff in 1972 was $157,092; for a senator, it ranged from $311,577 to $558,145, depending upon the size of the state. In the House, a member could hire up to sixteen staffers. In the Senate, there was no ceiling. A top aide to a House member could be paid as much as $30,600. The Senate ceiling was $35,742. If a member adds staff beyond the limits of the allowance, he must pay the excess out of his pocket.

What other allowances do senators and congressmen receive?

A House member is provided with an annual stationery allowance of $3,500; an annual postage stamp allotment of $910 for mailings other than those covered by the franking privilege, such as air mail and special delivery; 80,000 units annually for telephone and telegraph with each unit equal to a quarter minute of telephone time or one word in a telegram; $200 a month for the rental of district office space if a federal building is not available and up to $350 a month with the approval of the House Administration Committee; and a specified amount of office equipment. In the Senate, the annual stationery allowance varies from $3,600 to $5,000, depending upon the size of the state; up to $3,600 annually for office space in the state if federal facilities are not available; and $7,800 to hire staff to man the state office. Other allowances in the Senate are comparable to those in the House.

What kind of patronage does a congressman or senator have available to him?

Very little, really. Aside from his own staff, most members have virtually no jobs to dispense, unless they happen to be chairmen or ranking members of committees.

Can a senator or congressman also hold a position in the executive branch of government at the same time, such as secretary of state?

No. There is a specific prohibition against holding dual offices. In addition, no member of the House or Senate can be appointed to such a post if it is established during his term of office or to a position whose salary has been increased during that time. Exceptions have been made, however, to the latter provision when the member of Congress thus nominated agreed to serve at the previous salary level of the position. An example was the appointment of Congressman Donald Rumsfeld to head the Office of Economic Opportunity in 1969.

What's meant by congressional courtesy? Congressional immunity? What's the so-called "club rule"?

Congressional courtesy has two meanings.

The first relates to the relationship of the members to one another and to the entire body itself. They may never make personal attacks on colleagues which impugn their character or honesty. They also must abide by certain rules and customs to preserve the decorum and dignity of the chamber.

The result is that members generally are very cordial in addressing or talking about each other. This is true even in debates where they may disagree strongly. Occasionally, the decorum goes by the board, harsh words are exchanged and, once in a great while, fights break out.

But even then, the aftermath shows the effect of the courtesy rule. Thus, the *Congressional Record* rarely will carry any ungentlemanly remarks. They will be expunged during the editing of the record, a privilege the members have after they make oral remarks. Such editing frequently makes the *Record* interesting reading afterwards. The chopped-out sections sometimes join disparate parts together for an instant non sequitur.

Congressional courtesy also is a phrase used in replying to letters received from citizens in other states or congressional districts. The recipient member will not always reply but when he does he will inform the writer that "Congressional courtesy requires that I forward this letter to your congressman."

Congressional immunity is a limited protection from arrest for members while Congress is in session. The Constitution spells it out this way (Article 6, Section 1), "Senators and Representatives . . . shall in all cases, except treason, felony and breach of the peace, be privileged from arrest during their attendance at the session of their respective Houses, and in going and returning from the same." This has generally been construed to apply to immunity only when Congress is in session and when the member is on business of the Congress.

The so-called club rule is rather an amorphous state of mind which exists about Congress on Capitol Hill. It purports that members will close ranks to fend off any attack against the Congress as a whole or against their particular house, and this is usually the case.

The Senate is viewed as being more "clubby" than the House, having an inner circle or "establishment" of senior members who actually call the shots and control power. The House has a similar setup among the many little groups which exist within it. But the clubbiness in the House is more subtle and less detectable than in the Senate.

Who was the first woman elected to Congress?

Miss Jeanette Rankin, who was born in Montana in 1880, was the first woman elected to Congress, as representative-at-large from that state in 1916. A Republican, she served only one term but ran again and was elected in 1940. Interestingly, Miss Rankin voted against war with Germany in 1917 and was the only member of Congress to vote against entering World War II in 1941.

The second woman elected to Congress was Miss Alice M. Robertson in 1920. An Oklahoma Republican, she served only one term.

Who was the first woman to serve in the Senate?

Mrs. Rebecca Felton was the first to achieve that distinction, in 1922. She was appointed by the Georgia governor to succeed Sen. Thomas E. Watson, who died. Senator Walter George was elected on November 7, 1922, to fill out the term, but refrained from presenting his credentials until November 22, thus permitting Mrs. Felton to participate in the Senate sessions on November 21 and 22 and thus become the first woman to serve in the Senate.

The first female chosen for the Senate was Mrs. Hattie Caraway of Arkansas, elected on January 12, 1932. Both women were Democrats.

Can members of Congress be impeached?

It seems doubtful, although proceedings were instituted against a senator in 1798. Each house can, however, expel or censure a member with the concurrence of two-thirds of the membership. Congressmen and senators also are subject to prosecution in the courts for treason, felony, or breach of the peace, the same as private citizens.

CHAPTER 8

What about the presidency?

What's meant by the system of checks and balances? Does it really work?

It has worked for nearly two hundred years in this country, although sometimes imperfectly. Basically, checks and balances refer to the limitations imposed by the Constitution on the three branches of the federal government—the executive, the legislative, and the judicial.

Because the Founding Fathers feared an overconcentration of power in one single branch, they created all three separate and equal, each with some authority over the other. The president, for instance, can propose legislation to the Congress, which then may or may not act on it. He can also veto legislation sent to him, but the Congress can override his veto by a two-thirds vote of each house. The president can appoint federal judges, subject to Senate confirmation, but the Congress must appropriate the funds to run the judiciary as well as the other branches of government, including its own.

In *The Federalist No. 48*, James Madison confronted the question of checks and balances or separation of powers:

> It was shown in the last paper that the political apothegm there examined does not require that the legislative, executive and judiciary departments should be wholly unconnected with each other . . . unless these departments be so far connected and blended as to give to each a constitutional control over the others, the degree of separa-

tion which the maxim requires, as essential to a free government, can never in practice be duly maintained.

Although the question of balance between the president and the Congress has been with us since the beginning of the republic, it surfaced after World War II as the domination of the chief executive in the relationship began to wane. This was noted by George Galloway in his *History of the House of Representatives:*

> As the decade of the 1950s advanced, Congress reasserted its role in the formulation of public policy and showed promise of arresting the long-run trend toward executive leadership in policy formation. This shift seemed to be due to a variety of factors, including the division of the government between opposing parties, the apparent vacuum of leadership in the White House, the reorganization of Congress in 1946 and the streamlining of its committee structure, equipped with new professional staff aids and assisted by overall policy committees. Thus, policy formation became the product of the interplay of legislators, administrators and lobbyists acting under the apprehensive impact of a growing foreign menace on the threshold of the space age.

The process continued into the 1960s, with discernible shifts emerging in the balance of powers. The focal point in the late 1960s and early 1970s was the "undeclared war" in Vietnam, and a conscious effort developed to reassert the role of Congress in foreign affairs. Legislative proposals resulted, such as one to restrict the president from dispatching U.S. forces into hostilities abroad for longer than thirty days without specific congressional authorization.

In sum, the checks and balances written into the U.S. system nearly two centuries ago are alive and well.

Just how powerful is the office of the presidency?

The Constitution delineates the vast authority the chief executive has. He is the commander-in-chief of the nation's military forces. He is the country's chief of foreign policy and is empowered to enter into treaties with other nations with the consent of two-thirds of the Senate. He is empowered to appoint ambassadors, judges, and key officers of the government, again with the concurrence of the Senate in most instances. He has the authority to grant pardons or reprieves for specified federal offenses. He oversees preparation of the annual multibillion-dollar budget, by far the largest in the world, and its administrator once it has been approved by the Congress. In this nuclear age, he is the man whose finger is literally on the nuclear trigger.

In these and so many other ways, the presidency is beyond any other elected office in the United States in power and importance. But the powers he assumes do not make the president an ex officio success. As Richard E. Neustadt noted in *Presidential Power*, the chief executive is, institutionally speaking, more than two thousand people whom he has named to key posts in government. Neustadt pointed out:

> The President is only one of them. But *his* performance scarcely can be measured without focusing on *him*. In terms of party, or of country, or the West, so-called, his leadership involves far more than governmental action. . . . His strength or weakness, then, turns on his personal capacity to influence the conduct of the men who make up the government. His influence becomes the mark of leadership. To rate a President according to these rules, one looks into the man's own capabilities as seeker and wielder of effective influence upon the other men involved in governing the country.

The great power available to the occupant of the White House is only as good as its effective use through the sprawling network of the executive branch of government. He can preside, as in the sense of chief clerk, or he can lead, in the sense of chief executive.

What are the requirements to be president? Does the chief executive have to be born in the United States?

According to the Constitution, the president must be at least thirty-five years old, a resident of the United States for at least fourteen years and, technically, a natural-born citizen.

The question as to whether a child born abroad of American parents is a natural-born citizen in the sense of the specification has been debated frequently. The answer depends upon whether the definition of citizens of the United States in Section 1 of the Fourteenth Amendment is to be given an inclusive or exclusive interpretation.

The issue has never arisen regarding actual presidential nominees. However, it did come up prior to the 1968 Republican convention when then-Michigan Governor George Romney was a contender. He was born in Mexico of American parents. However, there was no final adjudication made of his status, although it was generally conceded that he would qualify if a test case were made.

How many American presidents were not born American citizens?

Eight of our presidents technically were British subjects since they were born before 1776. Included were the first seven presidents and the ninth chief executive, William Henry Harrison. Martin Van Buren, the eighth president, was the first who was at birth an American citizen. However, all were born in what became the United States.

What's the best stepping-stone to the presidency—the governor's chair or the Senate? Or is there another?

There is no one best stepping-stone any longer.

Immediately following the American Revolution, the stepping-stone seemed to be the office of secretary of state, the vice-presidency, and being a native of Virginia.

In the last forty years, the statistics produce a mixed bag. Three of our presidents had been vice-presidents. They also had been senators. They were Richard M. Nixon, Lyndon B. Johnson, and Harry S Truman. The late President John F. Kennedy had been a senator as well as a member of the House. Nixon and Johnson had also been House members at one time. But Presidents Franklin D. Roosevelt, who had been governor of New York, and Dwight D. Eisenhower had served neither in the vice-presidency nor the Congress.

The present pattern suggests that the Senate is the greatest spawning ground of presidential hopefuls, particularly in light of the senatorial background of the leading Democratic candidates in 1972.

Which state has had the greatest number of native-born sons become president?

Virginia, sometimes called "the Mother of Presidents," holds that distinction with eight, followed by Ohio with seven. The Virginians were Washington, Jefferson, Madison, Monroe, William Henry Harrison, Tyler, Taylor, and Wilson.

What's the difference between native son and favorite son?

A native son is a presidential candidate who was born in the state, while a favorite son is one who is his state's choice at his party's nominating convention. Quite often, a favorite son is a governor who is not a serious presidential contender but who keeps his state's delegation committed to him for trading purposes at the convention.

Unlike a native son, a favorite son doesn't have to be born in the state.

What's the background of U.S. presidents—law, business, teaching, journalism, or what?

The law predominates. Some twenty-four of the thirty-six presidents were members of the bar and practicing attorneys. Three were soldiers and farmers: Washington, Harrison, and Taylor. Three were writers or newspapermen: Theodore Roosevelt, Harding, and Kennedy. Two were solely military men: Grant and Eisenhower. Andrew Johnson was a tailor, Hoover a mining engineer, Lyndon Johnson a teacher, and Truman a farmer and haberdasher.

Three had experience as naval officers: Kennedy, Johnson, and Nixon —and twenty-one of the remaining thirty-three had some military experience. James A. Garfield, the twentieth president, was a lay preacher of the Disciples of Christ, but no chief executive has been an ordained minister or priest.

What are the odds on an incumbent president being reelected?

Two to one. Prior to the 1972 election, fourteen presidents seeking reelection made it, and seven were defeated. The losers were John Adams (in 1800), John Quincy Adams (1828), Martin Van Buren (1840), Grover Cleveland (1888), Benjamin Harrison (1892), William Howard Taft (1912), and Herbert Hoover (1932). Interestingly, although Cleveland was defeated in his second term bid in 1888 by Harrison, he came back to beat Harrison in 1892.

Has an incumbent president ever been denied renomination by his party?

Yes, these five failed to be renominated: John Tyler (1844), Millard Fillmore (1852), Franklin Pierce (1856), Andrew Johnson (1868), and Chester Arthur (1884). All except Pierce had been vice presidents who had succeeded to the presidency upon the death of the incumbent.

Which presidents won reelection to second terms prior to 1972?

They were George Washington, Thomas Jefferson, James Madison, James Monroe, Andrew Jackson, Abraham Lincoln, Ulysses S. Grant, Grover Cleveland, William McKinley, Theodore Roosevelt, Woodrow

Wilson, Calvin Coolidge, Franklin D. Roosevelt, Harry S Truman, Dwight D. Eisenhower, and Lyndon B. Johnson. Cleveland was elected twice but not consecutively, and FDR won four consecutive terms, breaking the traditional two-term limit.

How many vice-presidents have made it to the presidency? How many of those who took office because of the death of the president subsequently were reelected in their own right?

Twelve vice-presidents have become presidents. Only three who ran for the presidency while in the no. 2 position were successful. They were John Adams, Thomas Jefferson, and Martin Van Buren.

Eight vice-presidents became president due to the death of the incumbent. Four of them were nominated and elected to the next succeeding term: Theodore Roosevelt, Calvin Coolidge, Harry S Truman, and Lyndon B. Johnson. Richard Nixon, elected in 1968, is the only former vice-president to become chief executive.

When did the two-term presidential limit go into effect?

In 1951, with adoption of the Twenty-second Amendment to the Constitution.

How important is the vice-presidency?

It's as important as the president wants it to be. In the past, the vice-president was used mainly for ceremonial occasions, representing the president when he was unable or unwilling to appear and serving as presiding officer of the U.S. Senate, casting the deciding vote in the case of ties.

More recently, the office has become the stepping-stone for the presidency. The last four vice-presidents—Harry Truman in FDR's Administration, Richard Nixon in the Eisenhower Administration, Lyndon Johnson in the Kennedy Administration, and Hubert Humphrey in LBJ's Administration—have all become presidential contenders. Three of the four eventually won the presidency. The sole loser was Humphrey.

What functions does the vice-president perform?

His role is very limited constitutionally. He presides over the U.S. Senate and will become chief executive in the event that the president dies, resigns, becomes incapacitated, or is removed from office.

In the latter half of the twentieth century, it has become customary for presidents to delegate responsibilities to their vice-presidents, such as serving as chairman of certain councils, representing the president at various functions, and so forth. But these assignments are made by presidents individually.

Humorist Will Rogers once commented that the principal function of the vice-president is to inquire daily about the president's health.

When did the parties start holding national conventions to select presidential candidates?

Since 1832, all nominations for president and vice-president have been determined at conventions. The pattern was established in 1831 when the Anti-Mason party nominated William Wirt for president and Amos Ellmaker for vice-president in Philadelphia. That meeting was the first time a grouping of delegates representing the people convened to select candidates for the top national offices.

Since the Democrats were out of the White House between 1968 and 1972, why did they wait until 1972 to start building up a presidential candidate? Why wait for the national convention to decide, in other words?

It doesn't work that way. Until the party's national convention decides on its presidential nominee, the official party apparatus remains as neutral as it possibly can.

The building up is the responsibility of the would-be nominees themselves. The time between the preceding presidential election and the next nominating convention permits hopefuls to work on their candidacies. For instance, after the 1956 election was over, John F. Kennedy began to make plans to capture the 1960 Democratic presidential nomination, establishing a campaign organization and quietly launching his campaign several years ahead of the convention itself. The same thing happened in advance of the 1972 convention. In fact, Sen. George McGovern (D–S.D.) publicly announced his candidacy for the nomination well over a year and a half before the convention, where he won his party's nomination.

Is it actually necessary to hold a presidential convention every four years? Why?

Yes. Party rules not only require such a convention be held every four years but most state laws say that only presidential and vice-presidential candidates nominated by convention will be permitted to have their names placed on the general election ballot.

Are conventions regulated by federal or local laws?

Neither. They are the creations of their political parties, and federal or state laws have no more control over them than over a local American Legion meeting.

How is it decided whether the Republicans or Democrats will hold their national conventions first? How is the convention city selected?

Until recent years, it had been the custom for the Republican party to hold its convention at an earlier date than the Democratic convention. That custom has gone by the boards, however, and there are now no hard-and-fast rules.

Ordinarily, the party out of power holds its convention first on the theory that an early nomination will enable it to conduct a longer campaign to build up its candidate, who presumably would be lesser known than the president he will be running against. Thus, the 1972 Democratic convention was held in July and the Republican convention six weeks later in August.

The convention site is selected by party committees specially established for this purpose. Interested cities submit bids to the Site Selection Committees which screen them as to capabilities, including convention facilities, housing, and other accommodations. Each interested city usually submits as part of its bid a guarantee of funds to help the party underwrite convention costs.

The Site Selection Committee makes its recommendation to the party's national committee which usually ratifies the choice. If the party has an incumbent president in the White House, he is consulted as to his wishes, which usually prevail.

How are the delegates to the presidential nominating convention of the major parties selected?

There are several ways, of which the major ones are the caucus–convention method and the presidential primary.

In most states, the parties name the delegates directly by means of state conventions or the state committees. In effect, the selections are made by a caucus of the party leadership which includes representatives of local party organizations.

The district delegate system is used in about one-third of the states. The frame of reference is the congressional district. The delegates are selected through the party machinery and frequently are listed on the primary ballot.

While there are contests in some cases, the opposite is more generally true, and the participation of the electorate is minimal.

How many delegates were at the 1972 Democratic and Republican conventions?

The Democrats had 3,016 delegate votes at their convention and the Republicans 1,348. One vote over half in each case was needed to nominate.

How many of these delegates were elected in primaries and how many in state conventions or caucuses?

On the Democratic side, approximately two thousand were selected either directly or indirectly by primary election. On the GOP side, some six hundred were elected in primaries.

Which states held presidential primaries in 1972?

Twenty-two states and the District of Columbia: New Hampshire on March 7; Florida, March 14; Illinois, March 21; Wisconsin, April 4; Massachusetts and Pennsylvania, April 25; District of Columbia, Indiana, Alabama, and Ohio, May 2; Tennessee, May 4; North Carolina, May 6; Nebraska and West Virginia, May 9; Maryland and Michigan, May 16; Oregon and Rhode Island, May 23; California, New Jersey, New Mexico, and South Dakota, June 6; and New York, June 20.

The option of holding primaries is up to individual state legislatures. Hence, the number can fluctuate every four years.

Are there different kinds of primaries?

Yes, there are two kinds of presidential primaries. The presidential preference primary decides which of the prospective candidates the registered voters of one of the major parties want as their nominee.

In delegation selection primaries, voters choose delegates to their party's national convention either by voting for a slate of delegates supporting one of the presidential hopefuls or for individual candidates. In other words, delegates may run pledged, unpledged, or favorable to a particular candidate. In some states, delegates may choose to support the winner of the statewide preference primary.

How important are the primaries in the presidential nominating process?

It depends on the circumstances. When he was in the White House in 1952, Harry S Truman described primaries as so much "eyewash"—at a time when he was being challenged and eventually defeated in the New Hampshire primary by an upstart senator from Tennessee named Estes Kefauver. Truman, however, had the last word. Controlling his party's apparatus, he was able to press the convention into nominating his choice, Gov. Adlai Stevenson of Illinois, over Kefauver who had won most of the primary contests he entered.

More recently, primaries have helped to make or break presidential candidacies, as 1972 demonstrated. In fact, with the recent convention reforms which give the rank-and-file delegates greater say over their party's nominee, primaries are expected to increase in importance in the presidential process. The establishment of a national primary system to select presidential candidates, which is under consideration, would add even greater import to this method of selecting nominees.

Are convention delegates bound to support the primary candidate who got the most votes in their state?

Depends on the state. In some states, delegates are committed to the primary winner on the first and sometimes the second ballot. In others, the primaries are advisory only, and delegates are uncommitted. In still others, delegates are bound to a candidate until he releases them.

That's not very specific. Which state primaries bind delegates and which do not?

Okay, taking the Democratic party's 1972 convention as an example, here's a breakdown: New Hampshire's eighteen delegates were bound for the entire convention to the candidates they were pledged to; Florida's eighty-one delegates were bound on the first two ballots only (unless the candidate received less than 35 percent of the votes needed for nomination and, if so, they were released); Illinois' 170 delegates were not legally bound at all; Wisconsin's sixty-seven were bound until the candidate received less than one third of the convention votes; Massachusetts' 102 delegates were bound only on the first ballot; out of Pennsylvania's 182 delegates, 137 were bound on the first ballot; Alabama's thirty-seven delegates were not bound at all; the District of Columbia's fifteen were bound on the first two ballots; Ohio's 153 were not legally bound; and out of Tennessee's forty-nine delegates, nine were bound on the first ballot and forty on the first two ballots (unless the candidate received less than 20 percent of the convention votes).

In addition, North Carolina's sixty-four delegates were bound on the first ballot; out of Nebraska's twenty-four delegates, twenty-two were bound on the first two ballots (unless the candidate received less than 35 percent of the votes needed for nomination), and the remaining two were not bound at all; Michigan's 132 were bound for two ballots; Maryland's fifty-three were bound for two ballots (unless the candidate received less than 35 percent of the votes needed); Oregon's thirty-four delegates for two ballots; Rhode Island's twenty-two for the first ballot; California's 271 until the candidate received less than 15 percent of the votes cast; South Dakota's seventeen were bound for three ballots (unless the candidate received less than 35 percent of the votes); New Jersey's 109 delegates were not legally bound; New Mexico's eighteen were bound for the first ballot; and New York's 278 were not legally bound at all.

In the case of the 1972 Democratic convention, however, most of the above rules were academic since Senator McGovern won the nomination on the first ballot.

Are delegates' expenses paid to the national conventions?

No.

What's the "two-thirds rule" at national conventions? Is it still used? What's the unit rule? Is it still in effect?

The two-thirds rule no longer exists except as the vote required to suspend the rules at national conventions. In its earlier usage, the rule meant that a two-thirds majority of the delegates was required for the nomination of the presidential and vice-presidential candidates. The Democrats used this procedure up until 1936, when they went over to the simple majority procedure which the Republican conventions had employed since 1856. In some of the early Democratic conventions in the nineteenth century, the rule was viewed as a force for party unanimity.

The unit rule at presidential conventions required that the entire vote of a state delegation be cast for the candidate preferred by the majority of that delegation. For example, a state with twenty-five votes would have to give all of the votes to the candidate preferred by thirteen members of its delegation. The Republicans abandoned the unit rule in 1880, and the Democrats voted not to enforce the procedure at their 1968 convention.

Which president was nominated over opposition of a majority of the delegates from his home state?

Franklin D. Roosevelt, who was nominated at the 1932 Democratic convention in Chicago with two-thirds of his New York state delegation recorded against him on every roll call and in favor of Alfred E. Smith.

Interestingly, FDR's nomination set off such deep party resentments that he became the only Democratic presidential nominee in modern times denied the courtesy of a unanimous convention vote.

What happens if no winner emerges after the first few ballots at the convention? Do they keep going?

Since the chief purpose of the convention is to select a nominee for the party, the delegates continue voting until a standard-bearer is decided upon.

In 1924, it took the Democrats 103 ballots to nominate John W. Davis for president. But in recent years, most candidates have been nominated on the first ballot due chiefly to preconvention primary victories and effective delegate-hunting activities.

Who was the first black to serve as a chairman of a national political convention?

Blanche Kelso Bruce, a Negro senator from Mississippi, served temporarily in that capacity at the Republican National Convention in 1880. Eight years earlier, three Negroes made speeches from the rostrum as delegates to that meeting.

In 1884, a black was temporary chairman and keynoter of the Republican convention. He was John Roy Lynch, a former three-term member of the House of Representatives.

Can a candidate run for president and Congress at the same time?

Yes, unless the laws of his state prohibit it. But a candidate may not run for the Senate and the House concurrently.

The reason relates to a technical difference in the manner in which the executive and legislative branch candidates are elected. Members of Congress are selected by popular vote on the November election day. But the president and vice-president are determined when the electors cast their ballots in December.

Further, unless his state's law prohibits it, a sitting member of the Senate can be a presidential or vice-presidential candidate without having to resign his seat. With House members, the parallel does not exist since their terms are only two years, and they have no opportunity to run in midterm as do senators whose terms are six years.

If a presidential candidate dies or withdraws before the election, how is his replacement chosen?

The successor would be named either by the party's national committee itself or by a convention called together by the committee for that purpose. It most probably would be the committee's decision if the time for election were relatively close.

In only three instances has this type of problem presented itself and then only with respect to the vice-presidential candidate. The Democratic nominee for vice-president in 1844 declined after he was nominated, and the Democratic National Committee named a successor. In 1912, Republican Vice-President James S. Sherman died while running for re-election and the Republican National Committee picked a replacement to run with President William Howard Taft. In 1972, the Democratic National Committee met to select a replacement for vice-presidential candidate Thomas F. Eagleton, who resigned from the ticket following public disclosure of previous psychiatric treatment.

What happens if the president-elect dies before he's sworn into office but after his election?

The vice-president-elect assumes the place of the president-elect just as he would if the president were to die after being sworn in. The provision is contained in the Twentieth Amendment to the Constitution.

Can I vote for president and vice-president separately?

No. They run as a pair, and it is impossible to split the vote.

What is the Electoral College? How does it function?

As specified in the Constitution, the president and vice-president are elected to office by members of the Electoral College who are, in reality, slates of electors selected by voters in each state.

As out of keeping as it may seem today, the Founding Fathers were apprehensive about providing for the direct election of the chief executive. Alexander Hamilton recommended the electoral college idea, and it was adopted.

In most states, the names of the electors are not listed on the ballot. Instead, the voters see only the names of the actual candidates. In other states, a combination of the candidates and the electors appears. And in a handful of others, only the electors are on the ballot. The procedures are determined by the individual states.

The electors formally cast their ballots on the Monday following the second Wednesday in December in their respective state capitals. At that time, the electors who won cast all of that state's electoral votes for that party's presidential and vice-presidential candidates. In effect, it is a winner-take-all proposition since the votes for the parties receiving less than a majority simply are not figured into the result.

The results of the balloting of the electors in each of the states and the District of Columbia are counted officially in the U.S. Capitol on January 6 following the election by the president of the Senate in the presence of the House and Senate. Only after the president of the Senate announces the count is the president of the United States legally elected.

How are electors chosen?

It varies by states. In some, electors are nominated in primary elections. In others, they are appointed by state party conventions or by state committees of the political parties. Each state has as many electors as its total of U.S. senators and congressmen.

How many electoral votes are there? How is the total computed?

The total is determined on a state-by-state basis. The total number of representatives is added to the two senators from each state to arrive at its total electoral vote. The state of Vermont, for example, has one representative and two senators. Thus, it has three electoral votes. The state of Ohio has twenty-three representatives (beginning with the Ninety-third Congress in January 1973) and two senators for a total of twenty-five electoral votes. The Twenty-third Amendment to the Constitution adopted in 1964 gave the District of Columbia three electors.

Thus, the national total is 538, and a winning presidential candidate must receive not less than 270.

What happens if no candidate receives a majority of the electoral votes? Has this ever happened?

With no majority, the House of Representatives then decides which candidate shall become president. In this instance, each state has one vote. In other words, the representatives from each state vote among themselves to determine which candidate will receive that one vote. Then the balloting takes place in the House with a roll call of the states. The Constitution requires that the three candidates with the highest number of electoral votes be considered by the House.

Two presidents have been selected in this unusual manner. They were Thomas Jefferson in 1801 and John Quincy Adams in 1825.

In the case of the vice-president, when there is an absence of an electoral majority, the Senate makes the selection. In this case, the senators vote individually, considering the top two candidates for vice-president. The situation has developed only once, in 1837 when Martin Van Buren was elected president and the Senate chose the vice-president, Richard Johnson.

If the presidential race is thrown into the House of Representatives, does a lame-duck Congress after the election decide the winner or is it the new House which convenes the following January?

The lame-duck Congress—the one whose term ends in the January after the November presidential election—has no role whatever in selecting the president in the event that none of the candidates receives a majority of the electoral votes. The new, incoming House of Representatives has the responsibility. Their votes are cast by states, with one vote per state. Only the three candidates receiving the largest number of votes are in the running.

Are the electors bound to follow the preference of the voters?

In some states, the electors are bound by law; in others, it is merely customary that they follow the dictates of the electorate.

The Supreme Court has held that states can require a pledge from electors that they will vote for their party's candidate. But in states where there is no law, it is theoretically possible for the electors to exercise their own preferences.

Have any presidents been elected with a majority of the electoral votes but with less of the popular vote than one of the other candidates in that race?

It has happened twice in our history. In 1876, Rutherford B. Hayes polled 4,036,298 popular votes and a majority of the electoral votes, while Samuel Tilden drew 4,300,590 popular votes and went down to defeat. In the 1888 election, Benjamin Harrison had fewer popular votes than Grover Cleveland, 5,439,853 versus 5,540,309, but had enough electoral votes to gain the White House.

What happens if the president resigns, dies, or is incapacitated?

The vice-president assumes the powers and duties of the presidency in those circumstances.

The line of succession after the vice-president is the Speaker of the House, the President Pro Tempore of the Senate, and then certain members of the cabinet beginning with the secretary of state.

How is the office of the vice-president filled if he should die or resign?

The Twenty-fifth Amendment to the Constitution specifies that the president must nominate a successor who must be confirmed by a majority vote of both houses of Congress.

How many presidents have died in office? What is the "fatal 20s theory"? Is there anything to it?

A total of eight presidents have died in office.

Seven of the eight fit into the "fatal 20s theory." The theory, or pattern really, is that presidents elected every twentieth year ending in zero since 1840 have died in office. Only one chief executive who died while in the White House was not elected in one of the twentieth years. He was Zachary Taylor, elected in 1848 and deceased in 1850.

The presidents who have fallen victim to the "fatal 20s theory" and the years they were elected follow: William Henry Harrison, 1840; Abraham Lincoln, 1860; James A. Garfield, 1880; William McKinley, 1900; Warren G. Harding, 1920; Franklin D. Roosevelt, 1940; and John F. Kennedy, 1960.

The "fatal 20s theory" was started when this man, William Henry Harrison, was elected President in 1840 and died in office 31 days after being sworn in. Under the fatal 20s theory, presidents elected every twentieth year ending in zero have died in office. They were: Harrison, elected in 1840; Abraham Lincoln, 1860; James A. Garfield, 1880; William McKinley, 1900; Warren G. Harding, 1920; Franklin D. Roosevelt, 1940; and John F. Kennedy, 1960. The next election to test the "theory" will come in 1980. *From the Collections of the Library of Congress.*

Which presidents were assassinated?

There were four: Lincoln, Garfield, McKinley, and Kennedy.

Which president served the shortest time in office? Which the longest?

The shortest tenure was that of William Henry Harrison, who died thirty-one days after being sworn in. The longest was Franklin D. Roosevelt, the first chief executive to break the two-term tradition prevalent up to that time, who was reelected to a third and fourth term.

Where did the term "dark horse" start? "Stalking horse"?

A "dark horse" is a candidate who is considered to have little or no chance of winning his party's presidential nomination.

James Knox Polk is considered the first dark horse candidate to win the presidency. He managed to win the Democratic nomination in 1844 after a deadlock developed between former President Martin Van Buren and Lewis Cass. While Van Buren received the majority of the votes, he could not achieve the required two-thirds. Although well known to most politicians, Polk was a surprise to the country.

The term "dark horse" originated in British racing slang. It meant a horse about which little was known prior to race time. It also referred to the practice of attempting to disguise the appearance of well-known racers by dying their hair black and entering them under different names.

A "stalking horse" is the derivation of a hunting term. In the sixteenth century, bird hunters stalked their prey by walking behind horses, since wildlife do not usually become alarmed by the presence of another animal.

In politics, a stalking horse is a candidate who has no hope of winning himself but acts in behalf of another candidate, usually to split the opposition.

What's meant by a Sherman-like statement?

It's used as one of the best examples of absolutely declining to run for office as contrasted with those which leave the door to candidacy at least ajar.

The statement was made by Gen. William T. Sherman in 1884 when he was under pressure to run for the Republican nomination for president. Then retired from the Army, Sherman sent the convention chairman the following telegram: "If nominated, I will not accept; if elected, I will not serve."

How about age? Who have been our oldest and youngest presidents?

The oldest was Andrew Jackson. He was almost seventy when he ended his second term and almost sixty-two when inaugurated on March 4, 1829.

The youngest was Theodore Roosevelt. He was forty-two when he assumed the office after President McKinley was assassinated in 1901. When reelected in his own right in 1904, he was just forty-six years of age. President John F. Kennedy was the youngest man elected president, however. He was forty-three when he took office on January 4, 1961.

Who was the first Catholic nominated for president?

Long before the nomination of Catholics Alfred E. Smith of New York in 1928 or John F. Kennedy of Massachusetts in 1960, a faction of the Democratic party meeting in separate convention in 1872 nominated a New York Catholic named Charles O'Conor. Both O'Conor and his running mate, John Quincy Adams, grandson of the former president, declined the nominations. However, no replacements were nominated and O'Conor–Adams were listed on the ballot in twenty-three states as candidates of the Straight-Out Democrats as well as the Reform Labor party which also endorsed them. However, the ticket garnered only 29,000 votes.

Has a woman ever run for president of the United States?

Yes, several. The first was Mrs. Victoria Claflin Woodhull, who received the presidential nomination in 1872 from an organization which called itself the Equal Rights party. Running with Frederick Douglass, the noted Negro reformer, she received only a few thousand votes. She became a candidate again in 1880 and 1892. Having married a British subject in 1883, she actually was living in England when she ran for her third and last time. In 1884 and 1888, the Equal Rights party again nominated a woman for president—Belva Ann Bennett Lockwood.

Years later, in 1952, an organization calling itself the Washington Peace party nominated Linea W. Johnson for president. The first woman to seek the nomination of one of the two major parties was Sen. Margaret Chase Smith of Maine, whose name was placed before the 1964 Republican National Convention in San Francisco.

The first woman to seek the Presidency was Victoria Claflin Woodhull, who was nominated by the Equal Rights party in 1872. Her running mate was Frederick Douglass, noted Negro reformer. She received only a few thousand scattered votes. *From a Matthew Brady Photograph in the New York Historical Society.*

Which presidential election did women first vote in?

The first presidential year in which women used the right to vote was 1920.

The Nineteenth Amendment to the Constitution was the enabling enactment. Passed by the Congress on June 4, 1919, it was ratified by the necessary three-fourths of the states to become effective on August 26, 1920.

The amendment did not specify that women had the right to vote but prohibited discrimination against citizens on the basis of sex with respect to laws concerning qualifications for voters.

Can the president and vice-president be residents of the same state?

There is no constitutional prohibition against the two officeholders being from the same state, but Article XII of the Bill of Rights prohibits the electors of a state in which both candidates reside from casting their ballots for both of them: "The Electors shall meet in their respective states and vote by ballot for President and Vice President, one of whom, at least, shall not be an inhabitant of the same state with themselves. . . ."

Thus, if two candidates were nominated from the same state and received the plurality of the votes in that state, only one of them could be voted for by the electors.

The point is largely academic, however. Politics being what it is, only a most unusual set of circumstances could produce a ticket of the presidential and vice-presidential candidates being from the same part of the country, let alone residents of the same state.

Which is better—to have a president from one party and a Congress from the other or to have both branches controlled by the same party?

It depends on where you're sitting. If your party controls the national administration, you'll argue that it makes most sense to have a Congress of like persuasion. And in a sense it does, enabling a chief executive not only to set forth his proposals for legislation but to have a friendly legislature on hand to follow through on their enactment.

If the opposition party controls the administration, however, you'll argue that it's important to have control of Congress in the hands of your party to make sure the executive branch undergoes close scrutiny of both its programs and its habits. And there's validity to this argument as well.

Although the first presidential election in which women voted was in 1920, following adoption of the Nineteenth Constitutional Amendment, a number of territories and states had earlier enacted laws extending suffrage to women in state and local elections. The Territorial Legislature of Wyoming granted women the right to vote in 1869 and incorporated this right in its constitution when it became a state in 1890. Other states followed suit. This scene shows women lining up to vote in Cheyenne in 1888. *From the Collections of the Library of Congress.*

Ideally, a president should have a Congress controlled by his party for at least the first two years of his four-year term to help get his programs underway. And most presidents do. The election of President Nixon in 1968 was one of the few exceptions to this rule.

What's the presidential "coattail" theory? Is it valid? How does the size of a presidential candidate's vote affect the congressional races?

The "coattail" theory holds that a popular presidential candidate can bring into office with him congressional and other candidates from his party who otherwise might not be able to poll enough votes to win on their own.

Although there are numerous examples of this theory working, there are several instances where it hasn't. For instance, when Democrat Lyndon Johnson won a landslide election in 1964 over Barry Goldwater, he helped his party attain a net gain in the House of thirty-seven seats. Yet, eight years earlier in 1956, when Dwight D. Eisenhower was reelected in a landslide over Adlai Stevenson, the president's party lost two House seats.

In general, however, the presidential candidate who draws a heavy vote in state and congressional districts will also help his own party's candidates. Although the extent of this help varies, a rough rule of thumb is that the rise or fall by one percentage point of the presidential candidate in the final vote can affect as many as five of his party's seats in the U.S. House up or down.

How much support does the president get from members of his party in Congress? Do they vote right down the line with him? How about the Congress as a whole?

In the second session of the Ninety-first Congress, Republican President Richard Nixon was supported by Senate Republicans 60 percent of the time and by House Republicans 66 percent. By comparison, Senate Democrats went with him 45 percent and their House counterparts 53 percent. These support levels are fairly typical.

Under what circumstances can the president call a special session of Congress? When can he adjourn Congress?

The president's power to convene Congress, or merely one house, relates to "extraordinary occasions" and is specified in the Constitution.

Usually when this step is taken, the chief executive will identify the exact matter which needs the attention of the Congress. Once in session, however, Congress cannot be limited as to the subject matter it will consider.

The president's power to adjourn Congress applies to instances of disagreement between the two houses as to the time of adjournment. In such cases, the Constitution empowers the president to "adjourn them to such time as he shall think proper." No president ever has exercised this authority, however.

In addition to his salary of $200,000 annually, what other allowances does the president receive?

As a starter, the president has the use of a fully staffed White House, rent-free, as his official residence. Interestingly, the law technically allows him only the use of the furniture and other items owned by the nation which are present in the building.

The chief executive is authorized a $50,000 allowance for expenses incurred in his official duties. That sum is taxable. He also may expend up to $40,000 per year for travel and entertainment costs. That amount is not taxable.

In addition, the president has the use of military jets, helicopters, a yacht, limousines, a mountain retreat, secret service protection, and many other benefits.

If a price tag were put on all these benefits, how much would it total?

At least $9 million annually.

If the White House were put up for sale, what would be its estimated value?

Over $125 million for the building and grounds, according to some estimates.

How have presidents viewed their jobs?

Depending upon their temperament and makeup, they either like or despise the presidency. But nearly all who have served in that high office sought it eagerly in the first place and relished at least its prestige and power.

Nevertheless, from the time of George Washington, presidents have

"Why I would like to be President: I would like to be President so I could live in the White House and ride around in big cars and helicopters and have big banquets and get on television whenever I wanted to and be in motorcades and parades and have my picture taken all the time."

From New Yorker Magazine.

deprecated the job. The first president, who underwent unmerciful criticism and was even threatened with impeachment, once said, "I would rather be in my grave than in the presidency."

John Adams, who was a president himself and had a son elected to the same job, observed, "No man who ever held the office of president would congratulate a friend on obtaining it. He will make one man un-grateful and a hundred men his enemies for every office he can bestow."

Thomas Jefferson once declared, "No man will bring out of the presi-dency the reputation which carries him into it." Another time, Jefferson, who had previously served as vice-president, said, "The second office of the government is honorable and easy; the first is but a splendid misery." As he prepared to leave the White House, Jefferson commented, "Never did a prisoner released from his chains feel such relief as I shall on shaking off the shackles of power."

James K. Polk, who kept a diary on his presidential days, called the office "no bed of roses" and wrote as he departed from the White House, "I am sure I shall be a happier man in my retirement than I have been during the four years I have filled the highest office in the gift of my country." Polk died three months later.

When Abraham Lincoln came into the White House, his predecessor, James Buchanan, told him, "If you are as happy, my dear sir, on entering this house as I am in leaving it and returning home, you are the happiest man in this country."

Later, when a friend asked him how it felt to be president, Lincoln replied, "I feel like the man who was tarred and feathered and ridden out of town on a rail. To the man who asked him how he liked it, he said, 'If it wasn't for the honor of the thing, I'd rather walk.' "

James A. Garfield had this comment about the presidency: "My God, what is there in this place that a man should ever want to get in it." He was assassinated less than nine months later.

Grover Cleveland, embarking on his second four-year term, declared, "I look upon the next four years to come as self-inflicted penance for the good of the country. I see no pleasure in it." Later, after he had retired from the White House, Cleveland was asked how he felt with no official duties to perform. "I feel like a locomotive hitched to a boy's express wagon," he said.

Woodrow Wilson, whose two terms in office contributed to his physi-cal breakdown, once observed, "There are blessed intervals when I forget by one means or another that I am president of the United States."

Didn't any of the presidents enjoy their tenure in the White House?

Of course. Theodore Roosevelt was one president who thoroughly en-joyed his job. At one point, Roosevelt wrote to his son, Kermit, "I don't think that any family ever enjoyed the White House more than we have." Another time he observed, "I enjoy being president and I like to do the work and have the hand on the lever." After he left the White House, Roosevelt commented that he had "a corking good time" and added, "No president ever enjoyed himself as much as I have."

Franklin D. Roosevelt, although confined to a wheelchair, was so enamored of the job of president that he ran for the office and was elected to it four times. Eventually, though, the strain contributed to his deteriorating health and to his death.

More recently, such presidents as Harry Truman, Dwight D. Eisenhower, and Lyndon Johnson have all had their say about what has been called the "loneliest job in the world."

Upon assuming office on the death of FDR in April 1945, Truman told newsmen, "Last night the moon, the stars and all the planets fell on me. If you fellows ever pray, pray for me." Later, Truman remarked, "I've got the most awful responsibility a man ever had." But the cocky Missourian thrived on the presidency and won election on his own in 1948 against overwhelming odds.

General Eisenhower called the presidency "probably the most taxing job, as far as tiring of mind and spirit—but it has also, as I have said before, its inspiration." Later, discussing the powers of the presidency, Eisenhower said, "I believe that the problem of the presidency is rarely an inadequacy of power. Ordinarily, the problem is to use the already enormous power of the presidency judiciously, temperately and wisely."

President Johnson summed it up this way: "The presidency of this nation is no place for the timid soul or a torpid spirit. It is the one place where a petty temper and a narrow view can never reside. For the presidency is both a legacy from the past and a profusion of hope for the future."

Who is credited with saying "I'd rather be right than be president"?

Senator Henry Clay is usually identified as the source of that observation, although there is doubt as to whether he ever actually said it. As the story goes, Clay allegedly made the remark on the Senate floor after another senator had interrupted him with a pointed comment about Clay's presidential ambitions.

It's another one of those quotable quotes in American politics whose antecedents have become blurred.

CHAPTER 9

What's ahead?

What changes, if any, can be expected in the foreseeable future for the American political system?

Nothing drastic. Although there is unquestionably an evolution under-way in the American political process, which will continue through the 1970s, the evidence at hand suggests no major changes in the offing. True, numerous proposals have been made, ranging from limiting the tenure of the president and members of Congress to revisions in the actual electoral procedure itself. Some of these ideas will be incorporated into the system; others will not.

Congressman John Brademas (D–Ind.) put it this way in an essay he wrote for *The Future of the U.S. Government: Toward the Year 2000*:

"I do not think there will be a radical restructuring of American government between 1971 and 2000. The public is not that interested in political institutions, as distinguished from political issues, and any changes in the American Constitution are likely to be piecemeal."

This doesn't mean that the system will be unresponsive to needs. In fact, the contrary is more likely. For despite the slow and deliberate pace at which change takes place in a representative system of government such as that of the United States, the elements for action are more prevalent now than ever before—the disenchantment stirred up by U.S. involvement in an unpopular war in Southeast Asia, the discontent stimulated by the problems of the cities, and the distrust generated by the antiestablishment crusades of the young and others, not to mention the heavy and, in some cases, near-oppressive tax burden which cuts across most segments of society.

Thus, the very presence of these ingredients in ample quantity will serve as an accelerator toward the production of solutions. Writing in the same book from which Congressman Brademas is quoted above, James L. Sundquist comments:

> Alienation is present to some degree in all countries and at all times, but it waxes when institutions are rigid and it wanes when they respond. The characteristic of the American party system—in contrast, perhaps, to some of our other institutions—is its extraordinary flexibility. If we live now at a moment when our political institutions seem slow to respond to particular groups and grievances, we are looking at a circumstance that our whole political history suggests is transitory. As the pressure increases, the system does respond, because the people who are aggrieved possess the means, simply through participation, to see to it that it does.

It seems to me that the government can mitigate this feeling of alienation through its actions. Would you agree?

It's not that simple. By indicating its awareness of what disturbs the citizenry, however, by developing concrete actions which are visible, and by communicating its concern to the affected constituencies, the government can halt and even reverse the growth of alienation.

But the elected officials are not magicians, as Patrick Daniel Moynihan, advisor to presidents, once noted:

> Government cannot provide values to people who have none, or who have lost those they had. It cannot provide a meaning to life. It cannot provide inner peace. It can provide outlets for moral energies, but it cannot create those energies. In particular, government cannot cope with the crisis in values that is sweeping the western world. It cannot respond to the fact that so many of our young people do not believe what those before them have believed, do not accept the authority of institutions and customs whose authority has heretofore been accepted, do not embrace or even very much like the culture that they inherit.
>
> The 20th Century is strewn with the wreckage of societies that did not understand or accept this fact of the human condition. Ours

is not the first culture to encounter such a crisis in values. Others have done so, have given in to the seemingly sensible solution of politicizing the crisis, have created the total state, and have destroyed themselves in the process.

John Gardner, former secretary of the Department of Health, Education, and Welfare and now chairman of Common Cause, added this thought in his book, *No Easy Victories:*

> People who have never exercised power have all kinds of curious ideas about it. The popular notion of leadership is a fantasy of capricious power. The top man presses a button and something remarkable happens. He gives an order as the whim strikes him and it is obeyed.
>
> The capricious use of power is relatively rare except in some large dictatorships and some small family firms. Most leaders are hedged around by constraints—tradition, constitutional limitations, the realities of the external situation, rights and privileges of followers, the requirements of teamwork and, most of all, the inexorable demands of large-scale organization, which does not operate on caprice.

Specifically, what changes do you foresee? Let's take the role of political parties first. Are they on their way out?

No. Although the segment of voters who classify themselves as independents has risen in the past quarter century (from 20 percent to over 30 percent today, including the newly enfranchised eighteen- to twenty-year-old voters), political parties are not on their way out, in our opinion. In fact, concern for this trend away from party loyalty on the part of most voters has forced a reevaluation by the parties themselves of their political roles.

Both major parties have indicated the intent to bring independents who have defected back into the ranks. These efforts will take the form of expanded organizational activity from the national down to the local level, stepped-up public relations programs aimed at extolling the virtues of party identification and loyalty, and establishment of party-oriented training schools for full-time as well as volunteer workers. In fact, one plan under consideration is the establishment of a political "graduate school," sort of a "West Point of Politics," for young people who want to make careers of electioneering.

One significant analysis of the future of the party organizations was made by *Washington Post* political reporter David S. Broder, in his book, *The Party's Over*. Broder amplifies in one cohesive presentation many of the apprehensions of the late 1960s concerning the status of the national Democratic and Republican organizations and whether they are on the verge of extinction. The book's thesis, in brief, is that if the parties are done for, the consequences for the country will be substantial.

One salient consideration raised by Broder is the role of the party in determining policy. In reality, the president in office is the head of his party, and his positions become the party's policy. For the party not in power, the head is not always clearly distinguishable and, therefore, its stances frequently suffer from that fact.

But in the American system, as contrasted with the parliamentary, for example, positions are developed more by the individual officeholders than by the party as such. Ideological discipline of the sort evident in British politics is not the practice in the United States. Both major parties in this country, especially at the national level, contain a wide spectrum of philosophy from the extreme left to the extreme right, although the degree of extremity might be debated in some instances.

Thus, while there are philosophical differences between the two major parties, the brass ring of elective success both seek on the political carousel has been and will continue to be based more on the pragmatic than the ideological. The issue will not be so much whether a federal program ought to be established, but whether the solution to the problem at hand is the establishment of a federal program. The appeal to the voter will be in terms of solutions based on analyses of the factors bearing on the issues rather than any hard and fast commitment to a philosophical principle. If the position embraced dovetails with what is perceived as a party belief, then it will be so identified. But if it clashes with what previously had been construed as party doctrine, the plan, program, proposal, or bill will be advocated because it solves the problem. Perhaps the classic example can be found in President Nixon's welfare reform proposal. Essentially an evolutionary form of what was once called the negative income tax or the guaranteed annual income, the Nixon Family Assistance Program startled a number of Republicans, chiefly because it was a far cry from the traditional GOP approach to this problem.

In short, the practical bent of the parties is another cogent reason why they'll survive. After each defeat caused by philosophical dissensions in their ranks, the parties learn a little more about their chief mission in life, which basically is to elect those candidates who run under the party labels, regardless of whether or not they can pass an ideological litmus test.

Actually, what would happen if the two major parties simply went out of business?

The cause of responsible government would be seriously weakened. Instead of two major presidential candidates on the ballot, there could be half a dozen or more names. Instead of the two major parties running Congress, members of splinter parties and factions could be elected, forcing shaky coalitions and uneasy alliances to keep the government functioning. In short, the kind of constitutional crises which have faced France and other multiparty countries in the past could become a reality here.

Writing in the *Ripon Forum*, Howard L. Reiter discusses alternatives to the two party system in these terms:

> The more one becomes frustrated with the parties as they are, the more it becomes apparent that the only viable alternative is parties as they should be. A political system dominated by those who have no ties to parties, who wait until the next campaign to decide who is the best problem-solver, is a system rife with disaffection that spreads the more politicians try to overcome it.
>
> And it is high time that Americans stop being churlish about political power. To regard all of politics as corrupt *because* it involves power invites true alienation, i.e., dropping out, and keeps the misusers of power in office indefinitely. Let us recognize that to solve political problems requires giving political leaders the power to do so, which involves a commitment to parties entirely the reverse of the ticket-splitting trend.

I've heard talk about party realignments. Just what's meant by that?

Oversimplified, it means making one the Conservative party and the other the Liberal party.

The idea isn't new. Before he died in 1944, Franklin D. Roosevelt was reportedly considering throwing his immense prestige as president behind such a scheme. Others have proposed it from time to time with little success.

One argument against party realignment is that the wide spectrum of views now present in both parties largely precludes massive shifts in domestic and foreign policies which could result in changeovers from liberal to conservative administrations and vice versa. In short, the liberal–conservative membership span in each of the major parties today is a stabilizing force in keeping one or the other from tilting too far to the left or the right.

Is such a realignment likely to happen?

It's highly unlikely. For one thing, neither party has a hammerlock on the ideology represented by the designations liberal or conservative. True, the Republican party leans philosophically from the political center toward the right and the Democratic party toward the left, which means that both then battle for the middle ground in an election year, for that's where most of the voters are.

For another, the practical matter of making the transition from Republican and Democrat to the new alignment poses virtually insurmountable difficulties in terms of the officeholders. If the Democrats become the Liberal party, wholesale desertions could be expected by southern congressmen. Would the new Liberal, formerly Democratic, party be willing to accept the loss of an entire section of the country? We doubt it.

In sum, while the subject is discussed occasionally, the upheaval it represents is far too formidable to make the realignment plausible.

What about third and fourth parties? Are they going any place?

Probably not. For one thing, candidates from these parties tend to represent an extremely narrow point of view. Thus, they have difficulty in attracting a majority of the voters and have very little appeal for those in the middle-of-the-road category which comprises some 35 percent of the electorate.

To reach these voters, candidates from the far wings of the political spectrum sometimes move toward the political center, losing, in turn, support from advocates who first welcomed their candidacies because of shared political beliefs. As a result, much of their base support is eroded without real inroads being made into the middle.

Another reason for the lack of success of third or fourth party movements is the simple pragmatism of the two major parties. If a plank from a third or fourth party platform is popular, one or both of the major parties will probably incorporate it into their own. Witness the Democratic presidential candidates in the 1972 primaries who openly adopted George Wallace's tax relief issue, which was catching on with the voters.

There's still another factor. Even though many voters would like to support a third or fourth party contender, they fear this support could help to elect one of the major party candidates whom they really dislike. For this reason, many vote in general elections for the major candidate closest to their own political viewpoint. In fact, the Republican party capitalized on this concern of Wallace supporters in 1968 by warning that a vote for the Alabama governor was a vote for Democrat Hubert Humphrey. One indication that this appeal worked was the steady decline of Wallace support from a Gallup Poll high of 21 percent in mid-September to the 13.5 percent he finally obtained on election day.

What changes are expected in the makeup of the electorate?

A number. Looking ahead, the electorate will be younger, better educated, more affluent, and largely urbanized. It will be better versed on its public officials and demand more from them in the use of tax moneys and in the solution of problems.

Pollster Louis Harris made this point rather succinctly in a May 14, 1972, appearance on NBC-TV's *Meet the Press* in discussing changes in the electorate which had taken place between the 1968 and 1972 elections:

> I think there are profound changes taking place in our electorate and I think these have been basically under-reported. For example, there is a lot of talk about the youth vote going up—and it is going up from 18 to 23 percent. What isn't reported is that the number of college-educated people is going up 8 points, from 27 to 35 percent. What is not reported is that the number of voters in the $15,000 and over income is going up from 11 to 20 percent.
>
> What we find commensurately is that the so-called middle America is shrinking. The number of people whose education didn't go beyond the eighth grade is down five points. The number of people with incomes from $5,000–$10,000 is down 10 points just from 1968—so that the nature of the electorate for 1972 is almost totally different, I would say, from 1968, at least in terms of what makes a marginal difference in an election and what affects these people, these more affluent and young people—that is the vote for change in this country. So what we have is a deep undercurrent, which I think is going to grow rather than diminish, for change in terms of the American society. Not that people want to throw over the system—I think that is a mistake—but it is, rather, a feeling of "throw the rascals out" in terms of the people who are the leaders of our institutions in this country.

What about the so-called minority or ethnic voters? What role will they play in the years ahead?

One estimate is that there are as many as sixty-five million in the ethnic class, according to a 1972 study called *The Ethnic Factor: How America's Minorities Decide Elections,* by Mark R. Levy and Michael S. Kramer. These include the blacks; Spanish–Americans, including Puerto Ricans and Chicanos; Jews; Irish–Americans; Italian–Americans; the Slavs, embracing Poles, Czechs, Slovaks, the Ruthenians, Russians, Ukrainians, and others such as Hungarians, who are really not Slavic.

Although ethnic voters often tend to split their votes like any other group cross section of the country, they frequently come together when motivated and cast the bulk of the ballots for one candidate or the other. Take the 1960 presidential election, as analyzed by Kramer and Levy:

"In Texas, Chicano votes also made the difference, as the ticket was significantly aided by Texan Lyndon Johnson, a long-time friend of the Chicanos. Kennedy–Johnson did not win a majority in 'Anglo' precincts, but in Chicano neighborhoods, the ticket took a remarkable 91 percent of the vote (a 200,000 vote Chicano plurality as Kennedy–Johnson carried Texas by fewer than 50,000 votes)."

The other side of the coin was manifested in "three states, Arizona, California and Colorado, [where] Kennedy lost to Nixon by margins of 35,000 to 71,000 votes. Kennedy won substantial Chicano pluralities over Nixon in those states and at least 75 percent of the Chicano vote, but not enough Chicanos had registered (and voted) to tip the balance in Kennedy's favor."

Since the ethnic vote can be a factor in a number of states, it is something that presidential candidates can't write off and presumably will not in the years ahead. Such states as New York, California, Illinois, New Jersey, Ohio, and Pennsylvania, where there is a substantial number of ethnic votes, have 181 electoral votes, two-thirds of the total required for election.

What does the future hold for black political power? As the largest minority group, is its impact going to be any greater than it has been?

The potential definitely exists for the blacks to increase their influence. For example, in five states, they represent more than 25 percent of the population. These include Georgia, with 25.9 percent; Louisiana, 29.9 percent; Alabama, 26.4 percent; Mississippi, 36.8 percent; and South Carolina, 30.5 percent. In North Carolina, they are 22.4 percent of the population. And in five other states, they represent more than 10 percent of the people: New York, 11.9 percent; Illinois, 12.8 percent; Texas, 12.7 percent; Michigan, 11.2 percent; and Virginia, 18.6 percent.

Additionally, one-third of the entire black population lives in fifteen cities. In sixteen of the nation's cities, large and small, they make up more than 50 percent of the residents, and in fourteen others they comprise 40 percent.

The question then comes down to the elemental one of becoming sufficiently organized to register, turn out, and vote for a specific candidate. The blacks have done this on occasion, but they also have failed to do so, distracted in most cases by independent candidates, usually black, thus dispersing their power.

But as Levy and Kramer observe: "Leery of being used at election time by the major parties, the black leadership is struggling to mobilize its constituency effectively, to organize and hold blacks together in order to deal in the political power which is the currency of this nation. Accordingly, black leaders everywhere, wanting first to create a force to be reckoned with, echo Georgia legislator Julian Bond's warning that the black man has 'no permanent friends, no permanent enemies, just permanent interests.' "

Effectively marshalling this voting power, which has been enhanced by the enactment of voting-rights legislation, is the problem confronting black leaders. Evidence of attempts to achieve greater unity has surfaced in national black political conventions and meetings, and by extensive activity on the part of such groups as the Black Congressional Caucus, which comprises the thirteen black members of the House of Representatives.

Generally Democratic in their politics since the FDR era, the blacks were constant Republicans from Reconstruction up until the 1930s. Although they will give selected Republicans a good percentage of their vote —Dwight Eisenhower received 40 percent running for president in 1956, for example, and Winthrop Rockefeller 96 percent running as the successful Republican candidate for governor in Arkansas in 1966—the rule rather than the exception is to give the bulk of their votes to the Democrats.

Do you look for many changes in the conduct of campaigns?

Several. Since political campaigning is a specialized art, we look for an increasing number of specialists to enter the field, chiefly in the area of campaign management. This will develop, in turn, a professionalism which will, hopefully, help to remove some of the more irritating aspects of campaigning from public view, such as the endless speeches, bland TV commercials, cliché-ridden ads, all of which more often tend to madden than to motivate.

To curtail campaign costs, which are still out of sight despite federal limitations on media spending, we expect serious congressional consideration of legislation requiring radio and television stations to provide free time to candidates for federal office, presidential as well as congressional. We further look for Congress to eventually go along with the proposal for either free or reduced-rate mailings to help candidates reach the voters. Interestingly, one of the early proponents of free radio–TV time for candidates was the late President Eisenhower who urged that each station be required to give at least six half-hours of prime time to each major party presidential candidate to permit him to present his case to the public.

Because of the fatiguing aspects of the present presidential primary system, both on the candidates and on the public, we look for adoption of a national primary of some kind to select candidates for that office. A modification of the plan proposed by Senators Mike Mansfield (D–Mont.) and George Aiken (R–Vt.) or the one suggested by Sen. Robert Packwood (R–Ore.) would seem most likely. (See Chapter 9.)

In the funding of campaigns, the use of federal money to replace private contributions in national campaigns is a definite possibility. Although candidates would still be required to raise the money for their primary campaigns, such a system could help relieve candidates of one of their biggest headaches, once nominated. Interestingly, the tax checkoff idea isn't unique to the U.S.—West Germany, for instance, has had it in effect since the mid-sixties.

In the election of presidents, we look for the adoption in this decade of a constitutional amendment to change the methods of selecting presidents from the present winner-take-all electoral college system to either direct, popular election or a variation of the electoral college plan which would apportion electoral votes on the basis of a candidate's popular vote total. Such a change would affect the nature of presidential campaigning, with candidates concentrating less on the big population states with their large electoral votes and more on the one-man, one-vote aspects of the entire electorate.

What about the length of campaigns? Should they be shortened?

Yes, particularly the presidential campaigns. The availability of instant communications and the possibility of substantial free broadcast time eliminate the need for prolonged campaigns. In fact, we might well take a page from the British who limit campaigns to three weeks and thus spare their country the fatigue and frustration which characterizes the two- and three-month campaigns in this country, not to mention the primary campaigns which start in the preceding January or earlier.

One way to shorten campaigns would be for the two major parties to agree to schedule their conventions during the first two weeks in September, with the party out of power holding its conclave first. This by itself would force a curtailment in campaigning.

What about campaign financing? What would you identify in the way of possibilities?

As outlined in Chapter 6, the mechanism has been established for the federal financing of presidential campaigns. Beginning with income tax returns filed in 1973, taxpayers may check off $1.00 to be used in the 1976 presidential campaign. As we pointed out, however, these moneys would revert to the treasury for other uses if the Congress fails to take the required action formally appropriating the funds for this purpose or if the president vetoes the legislature's action.

Another possibility is the extension of the federal checkoff plan to congressional campaigns as well. In other words, the law might be broadened to cover campaigns for all federal offices—the presidency, the Senate, and the House. The cost of such a program, assuming two major party candidates for president and contests for all 435 House seats and 33 to 34 Senate seats, would be in the range of $100 million. This figure is based on the $.15-per-eligible-voter (140 million altogether) formula specified in the federal checkoff funding plan for presidential candidates, plus the addition of two candidates for each Senate and House seat.

Opposition to this plan clearly could arise on several bases. One is that both parties do not always field candidates for every House and Senate race. Thus, federal financing would provide an incentive which does not now exist for opposition in certain races. On an ideal basis, such a development is desirable. On a political basis, congressional incumbents could be expected to be less than enthusiastic about the federal government funding the campaigns of their opposition. Another objection could be on the grounds that the money could be better used for other worthy undertakings. In a sense, this contention may be correct. But $100 million in a federal budget of more than $200 billion is a small sum to pay for the election of candidates unfettered with massive campaign debts or unbeholden to special interests.

Will there be any changes in the federal elections law enacted in 1972? Are there any loopholes that need to be closed up?

Changes were proposed almost before the ink was dry and the legislation went into effect on April 7, 1972. The bulk of the amendment push was to loosen up the provisions of the law relating to filing deadlines and frequency.

Many congressmen, candidates, and contributors were annoyed at the detail required by the spending disclosure law. As a result, sentiment for simplification developed, and efforts will be made to achieve that goal.

There are loopholes in the present law. But, as an article in the *New Republic* of April 22, 1972, stated, "On balance, however, the Federal Election Campaign Act is more law than loophole," a takeoff on former President Lyndon Johnson's observation that the old law was "more loophole than law."

There are several means which legally may be used to avoid identifying an individual's contributions to a campaign. One acknowledged example is the so-called "check swap," the equivalent of earmarking the funds for a designated candidate. A committee or individual may wish to donate $500 to a candidate, but prefers to remain unlisted as a contributor. The check is made out to one of the major parties' committees, which deposits it and then, in turn, issues its own check directly to the candidate whom the contributor wants to get the money. Thus, the cancelled check of the contributor merely shows that it went to one of the established party committees.

Another approach is for an individual or organization to forward the check to a particular officeholder or candidate, made out to one of the party's campaign committees. The recipient then turns it over to the appropriate committee which issues its own check in the identical amount in return.

Since the law does not require reports from committees receiving or spending less than $1,000 in a calendar year, another way to avoid identifying contributors is to establish a series of these small campaign committees, thereby enabling donors to it to remain out of sight.

In addition to these legal loopholes, there also are other, clearly illegal ways of avoiding the reporting requirements. One is to donate cash and to have the recipient committee or candidate not list it at all. Another is the old standby of contributions in kind which are not reported. For example, a candidate's campaign committee arranges to have all of its direct mail handled by a company owned by one of the candidate's supporters who prefers not to have that service listed as a contribution. The company simply forgets about billing the candidate for the work performed. Still another old dodge is the technique of having a company or union billed for a campaign expense. Let's say the candidate has a big booster in the form of a local labor union in his home town. The union uses large amounts of mimeograph paper. During the election year, a portion of it is delivered to the candidate's headquarters instead of to the union hall. Still another is to distribute funds among friends for them to contribute in their names.

Since the legal as well as illegal loopholes so often defy fair and effective ways of closing them, the job before Congress in changing the 1972 law will be monumental. Odds are that only perfunctory, if any, revisions will be made.

In addition to closing some of the loopholes cited, what other changes are needed?

We feel that two major ones stand out.

The first is the establishment of an independent federal elections commission to oversee the compliance with the election law. Such a body was provided for in the Senate version of the campaign act. However, the House version of the bill specified "supervisory officers" rather than an election commission. The supervisory officers were the Clerk of the House of Representatives, the Secretary of the Senate, and the General Accounting Office. This provision prevailed during the House–Senate conference on the bill, and the idea of the commission was discarded.

At present, the Senate and House are responsible for the supervision of the campaigns of their own members, and the General Accounting Office for the presidential campaigns. The establishment of an elections commission would place that responsibility under a separate and independent agency with the authority to act as the facts dictate without concern about reactions from the executive or legislative branches of the federal government.

As proposed in the Senate bill, the commission comprised six members, "not more than three of whom shall be members of the same political party . . . appointed by the President with the advice and consent of the Senate." A full-time staff was envisioned for this board of directors, headed by an executive director. The commission would have broad authority to obtain the assistance, where required, of the Justice Department and General Accounting Office.

The second improvement that could be made is the establishment of the strongest possible penalties in the law for violations, including even that of disqualifying candidates for certain violations. In England, for example, if a candidate spends more than the law allows, the courts can impose heavy fines; if an overspender wins, his election can be nullified. A no-nonsense attitude thus would be demonstrated, and every individual who wishes to be a candidate for federal office would be compelled to be attentive to the requirements of the law.

This second proposal presupposes two factors: (1) that the law will be as uncomplicated as possible, something that was not generally conceded during its first year of use; and (2) that enforcement will be effected. Enforcement was perhaps the single greatest deficiency in the legislation that existed prior to enactment of the 1972 law.

There seem to be periodic discussions of doing something about election results being made public before all the polls have closed. The problem occurs primarily during presidential elections when returns from the East Coast appear on nationwide TV before the polls in the western states, including Alaska and Hawaii, have closed. What can be done about it?

It is doubtful that legislation banning the release of results could be passed or whether it would even be constitutional.

However, one approach which had merit was advanced by the GOP's 1964 presidential candidate, Barry Goldwater. Senator Goldwater suggested that the polls be kept open for a uniform 24-hour period throughout all fifty states. In other words, every polling place would open and close at the same moment regardless of time zone. In this way, ample time to vote certainly would be provided, particularly for persons who work unusual or irregular hours. Another factor could be quicker in-and-out voting since the lines of voters which frequently queue up at the polls would be largely eliminated.

At the present time, there is little impetus for any alteration of the existing system. We suspect that an unusually close presidential race whose outcome depends upon the results of the last few states may be required before sufficient momentum is generated to effect any such change.

Will the role of the president and the executive branch of government change in the years ahead? Can you visualize any significant shift in the president's power or authority?

No. There is little to suggest any substantive change in the office of the presidency.

As we have noted, there have been proposals to change the present two-term limit to that of one six-year period in office. But hardly any enthusiasm is evident on Capitol Hill and very little elsewhere to pursue it much beyond the discussion stage.

The president will continue to be the chief executive and the head of his party. He will continue to do battle with the Congress because of the built-in nature of the two institutions, much as the press and government have constantly confronted each other and will continue to do so.

In the final analysis, the presidency is as much or as little as the person holding it wants to make of it. He can be a placid president like Calvin Coolidge, who once commented about agriculture that "farmers never made much money anyway and there's not much we can do about it," to an activist like Franklin Roosevelt, who reshaped the parameters of presidential power in pressing for his objectives.

What's ahead for Congress? What type of representation will we get in the future?

If most of the other changes we discussed go into effect, including federal funding of U.S. Senate and House races, it should bring about a number of changes in Congress as well. For one thing, like the voters they will represent, the senators and representatives of the future will be younger, better educated, more affluent, and more urban-oriented.

Congressman John Brademas (D–Ind.) discussed some of the changes in his previously cited essay:

"As the nation grows younger and levels of education rise, the characteristics of senators and congressmen will change. Better-educated legislators will become more numerous and powerful in both parties, and they will tend to have fundamentally different perceptions of their roles than they do now. They will focus primarily on issues that cut across lines of geography and economic interest, problems that affect the entire country, and, indeed, the world."

At the same time, one-party domination of certain regions of the country, such as the South, will be replaced by a truly competitive two-party system which, in turn, will help to produce better representation in the U.S. Senate and House.

What changes do you foresee in Congress?

Aside from the wide-ranging proposals for reform which have been made—most of which are not in the immediate offing—two principal changes stand out.

First, Congress is on the verge of coming into the electronic age, with the installation of electric voting for the first time, and electronic data processing and automated equipment to speed the flow of paper work.

Second, because Congress now has one of the best retirement systems in the country for its members, more veteran members than ever are taking advantage of these increased benefits to retire into private life, thus reducing the age of Senate and House members and seniority starting with the Ninety-third Congress in 1973.

The first change will aid members of Congress in the performance of their duties, enabling them to better husband their limited time while infusing them with instant information on everything from programs in planning to policies in effect. The second provides Congress with an immediate injection of younger ideas and concepts which, in turn, could produce changes of their own.

What about the congressional seniority system? Will it be revised? What's the outlook?

There has been some effort to alter the traditional system of appointing committee chairmen and ranking minority members in the House and Senate, and the question was the subject of extensive debate in early 1971 with the start of the Ninety-second Congress.

The Senate considered but voted down a proposal whereby committee chairmen would be selected on a basis other than length of service. The House, however, did modify its procedures in separate actions taken by Republicans and Democrats in 1971, as noted in Chapter 7.

In January 1971, House Republicans, meeting in conference, voted authority to their Committee on Committees to recommend nominees for top House committee posts and to then submit these names to the House Republican Conference for approval by secret ballot. There was no requirement that the members recommended have the longest service. If the conference fails to approve any of the recommended nominees, the matter is automatically referred back to the Committee on Committees to come up with another selection.

House Democrats, meeting in caucus shortly thereafter, adopted a similar procedure under which their Committee on Committees would nominate the chairmen and membership for each House committee, but not necessarily on the basis of seniority. Additionally, upon demand of ten members, the nominations could be debated and voted upon. In the event a nominee was rejected, the Committee on Committees would then come up with another name.

All in all, these actions were a good start toward modifying the system under which length of service was the sole criterion for leadership positions on congressional committees.

What are the chances of action limiting the terms members of the Senate and House may serve?

Not very good, really. Since members of Congress would have to act on such a constitutional amendment, it is unlikely they would be inclined to place limits on their own job tenure. A more likely possibility would be an amendment precluding members of Congress or others from seeking election to the Senate or House beyond a certain age, such as seventy. This would serve much the same purpose as a term limitation.

Interestingly, one of the more unlikely advocates of a ceiling on congressional service was the late President Dwight Eisenhower, who proposed senators be limited to two six-year terms, or twelve years, and terms of House members be extended to four years from the present two years, and limited to three such terms, or twelve years total. Ike said such a plan would provide "a more rapid turnover of the membership in both houses with its constant infusion of new blood."

How about the urban–rural breakdown of the Congress? Will that change much?

Speaking more of the House than the Senate, the outlook is for a continuing increase in the representation of the nation's suburban areas.

The number of suburban congressional districts grew markedly between 1950 and 1970, rising from some 70 to nearly 150. By the year 2000, there may be as many as 250. At the same time, the central cities declined during this period. In 1950, approximately 110 congressmen were from central-city districts; by 1970, the total had dropped well below 100. This figure could be halved within the next thirty years. Similarly, rural areas, heavily represented with about 200 seats in the 1950 Congress, lost almost 30 percent of them to increasing urbanization by 1970. Sixty or seventy more could disappear by the turn of the century.

The significance of these changes is that the complexion of the House clearly will be largely urban/suburban, or even metropolitan if you will, within the next thirty years, possibly by as much as 6–1 or 7–1. Because of the tendency of rural and inner-city America to reelect their congressmen more readily than do the suburbanites, an interesting tug of war may be in the offing if the congressional seniority system is not altered in the meantime. In other words, rural congressmen who have retained their committee chairmanships would face the prospect of a Congress with an increasingly urban viewpoint.

The Senate, however, is not elected on the basis of population. Not conceived as representative of the country on a per capita basis, it has grown even less so and appears certain to continue that trend. Thus, the stage may be in the making for clashes between the House and Senate, particularly on matters relating to the cities and suburbs.

What about the presidential primary system now in effect? Will it be changed? If so, what kind of changes do you expect?

The public clearly has grown weary of the seemingly interminable primary election procedure for presidential candidates. The circus atmosphere surrounding the campaigns, not to mention the actual nominating conventions themselves, has gotten to the politicians as well as the voters.

A key development took place on March 13, 1972. On that date, Senators Mike Mansfield (D–Mont.) and George Aiken (R–Vt.) introduced a resolution for a constitutional amendment to establish a single national presidential primary day. Upon passage by the House and Senate and ratification by three-fourths of the states, the primary would be set for the first Tuesday following the first Monday in August of presidential election years.

Mansfield's remarks in behalf of the proposal were well-taken. Following the New Hampshire presidential primary, he noted, "A headline writer put it clearly: 'The Road Show Moves To Florida.' That caption said everything there is to say about the effect of the current system of presidential primaries upon the democratic processes of this nation." Mansfield continued:

> The truth is, the happenstance primaries have just begun and if everything goes as it has in the past, the results will never be in. Indeed, there will be no results. As in the past, no two of this year's primary tests offer the voter or the hopeful candidates any resemblance of popular opportunities. . . . In some states, what the voter faces is a long list of strange names and even stranger circumstances. The delegates he selects may go to a convention where votes are cast, not as the people back home prescribe, but in the manner a particular delegate himself happens to decide.

On April 12, 1972, House Republican Leader Gerald R. Ford introduced the identical resolution in the House, a strong indication of growing, bipartisan leadership support for change.

With the backing of key members of Congress, the single national presidential primary or some variation of it is an idea whose time has come. Ratification of the required number of states could occur in time for the 1976 election, which, appropriately enough, is the 200th anniversary of American independence.

How would the Mansfield–Aiken plan work? Would the winner need a majority of the votes cast?

The candidate receiving the greatest number of votes cast by registered voters of his party would become its standard-bearer, provided he received at least 40 percent of the total. If either or both of the parties failed to provide the required 40 percent plurality to any of its candidates, a runoff election would be conducted between the top two vote-getters of the party on the twenty-eighth day after the date of the primary election. Only persons eligible to vote in the primary election would be permitted to participate in the runoff.

To be listed on the primary ballot of all of the states, a major party candidate would be required to file petitions with the president of the U.S. Senate signed by a number of qualified voters equal to 1 percent of the votes cast in the last election for the presidential candidate of his party in each of seventeen states.

For candidates of minor parties—which did not have electors on the ballot in seventeen states but polled at least 10 percent of the vote cast nation-wide—the requirement would be 1 percent of the total vote cast throughout the United States in the last election.

Only persons registered by party affiliation could vote in the primary, and there could be no crossovers.

What are the pros and cons of the proposal for a single national presidential primary?

In addition to the argument that the present primary system leaves the public bored and bewildered and the candidates tired and broke, there are three reasons usually cited for adopting the single national primary plan:

1. The present system doesn't really prove anything. Because numerous candidates are entered, the parties' strongest contenders in the general election do not necessarily reflect that strength in the splintered primary elections. Thus, they are inconclusive.

2. The national conventions are generally run by the party's professionals who tend to ignore the results of the state primaries. Thus, the primaries are so much "eyewash," as former President Harry Truman once characterized them.

3. The crossovers from one party to another in primaries obscure the real result of the effort. In the 1972 Wisconsin primary, for example, a large number of Republicans reportedly cast ballots in the Democratic primary since President Nixon was virtually uncontested. Thus, the results are meaningless.

On the other side, the arguments usually cited for continuing the present system are:

1. The public has a better chance to size up the candidates. The months-long exposure to the electorate, because of the lengthy primary process, enables voters to make a better judgment of the candidates.

2. The parties' national convention can pick better compromise candidates than can party voters in a single national primary. Additionally, minority interests receive better attention in that environment.

3. The cost of a campaign for a single national primary election is prohibitive and would equal that of the general election itself.

Where does the public stand on the single presidential primary idea? Is the majority for it?

The proposal really is not new. Pollsters have tested public opinion on it as far back as 1952 when the idea first generated bipartisan backing. In that year, the Gallup Poll found the public favoring the plan by a margin of 6–1.

Twenty years later, in April 1972, the Gallup Poll again conducted a survey. The results showed the margin of support to be 4–1. Of note was the finding that 72 percent favored the plan while only 18 percent were definitely opposed and the remainder undecided. A breakout of the attitudes by party affiliation demonstrated general unanimity, indicating the nonpartisan nature of the issue. Those who considered themselves independents endorsed the change 77–17 with 6 percent undecided; Democrats were for it 72–17–11, and Republicans 66–23–11.

Is there any chance of the vice-presidential candidates ultimately being selected by means of a single national primary, possibly in conjunction with the nomination of the president, if that procedure is adopted?

It seems unlikely that the vice-president would be nominated in a national primary. One reason is that the field of candidates is considerably reduced under that concept. If an individual has presidential aspirations but no great prospect of winning the nomination, he nevertheless might enhance his chances for vice-president by a good primary showing. A vice-presidential primary would rule out that kind of chance and, in effect, restrict the system.

You referred earlier to a variation of the Mansfield–Aiken proposal. What kind of variation?

One possibility is the proposal of Sen. Robert Packwood (R–Ore.) which calls for adoption of an orderly pattern of regional elections to replace the state primaries. Packwood's plan would divide the country into five regions, each of which would conduct separate presidential preferential primaries on a staggered timetable. A five-man commission would be established to supervise this. The first election would be held on the second Tuesday in March and the other four on the same day in succeeding months. Lots would be drawn to determine the order in which the regional elections would be held.

As part of his plan, the senator would have convention delegates appointed by the winning candidates instead of having them elected. Delegate appointments would be based on the number of votes received by each candidate in that region's primary. For instance, a candidate who polled 40 percent of the regional vote would appoint 40 percent of the delegates. Delegates would be bound at the national conventions to stand by the candidates who appointed them for at least two ballots, unless released sooner, or unless the candidate received less than 20 percent of the vote on the first ballot.

The Packwood regional plan has certain advantages over the Mansfield–Aiken single primary proposal and vice versa. Since the single primary plan calls for a run-off if no candidate commands at least 40 percent of the vote, this could result, in effect, in three national elections, a costly venture in both effort and money. Packwood said his system would enable candidates who fail to do well in the first regional primary to back off from the remainder and cut their losses.

Columnist Kenneth Crawford, writing in the *Washington Post* in mid-1972, called the Packwood plan "the most plausible yet proposed for reform of the presidential primary election system—if it can be called a system."

Let's assume the idea of the single presidential primary is not adopted. What changes, if any, are in store for the nominating conventions?

The representation at the conventions, and therefore the methods of selecting the delegates, will be a major point of controversy.

The public saw the issue surface during the Democratic Convention of

Titled "Next!" this cartoon by Rube Goldberg depicts one of the more irritating aspects of national nominating conventions. The authors foresee shorter conventions ahead, less speech-making and more business-like conditions prevailing. They also look for changes in the electoral college system and in the manner of selecting presidential candidates. *From the Collections of the Library of Congress.*

1972 when the "Daley delegation," headed by Chicago Mayor Richard Daley, was disqualified by the credentials committee and the vote of the delegates. The problem was discussed cogently in Judith H. Parris' *The Convention Problem*, the highlights of which were summarized in Brookings Institution *Research Report No. 127* in 1972:

> Delegates to the 1968 conventions—and doubtless the earlier ones —were overwhelmingly affluent, white, male, and over thirty years of age. Both the electorate and the voters for Nixon and for Humphrey in 1968 included proportionately far more women, more nonwhites, more young people and more elderly people, and more persons of modest income than were included in the convention delegations. This pattern is unfair. As quasi-public institutions, the conventions should better reflect their own constituencies. Racial, sexual, age and income groups should be represented in the delegations in proportion to their share of the party's presidential constituency—the total electorate and the party's own voters.

Another improvement that Ms. Parris cites also has much to recommend it: "The trend toward bigger conventions should be reversed. In the interests of efficient deliberation, they should have no more than 1,500 delegates, fewer alternates, fewer other people in the hall, and smaller committees." Further, she urges:

> Rules should be adopted and enforced that would balance efficiency with the need to give each participant an opportunity for rational deliberative judgment. In other words, ordinary delegates should have time to read committee reports before voting, and those opposed to committee recommendations should have an opportunity to present a minority report to be voted up or down by the convention. Delegates seeking recognition ordinarily should arrange their motions with the chairman in advance; unless their requests are frivolous, they should be granted. Petition requirements and the rules for allocating speech time should be designed to discourage minor candidacies. Procedures such as the old unit rule, which inhibited delegates from voting as they wished, should be prohibited. Any delegate should be able to obtain a poll of his or her delegation, and roll call votes should be required at the demand of a substantial fraction of the delegates.

The thrust of Ms. Parris' analysis is that an across-the-board streamlining and improvement of the presidential nominating conventions is in order. In our view, the prospects for at least some revisions along the lines she proposes seem good.

Could conventions be eliminated entirely?

Not really. Conventions will be with us in some form or another for a long time to come, in our opinion.

Even if a single national presidential primary or something similar is adopted, thereby erasing some work of the quadrennial conventions, there would still be a need for such conclaves. For one thing, the conventions would still be called upon to select vice-presidential candidates, adopt the party's platform, and develop rules for the party for the next four years. Equally important in many respects, a convention provides the rallying ground for the party faithful from across the country and stimulates participation in the party system.

What about the Electoral College? Will it be abolished in favor of direct popular election of the president rather than continue the original procedure of electors and electoral votes?

We estimate that, by the end of this decade, the Electoral College either will no longer exist or will be modified to allocate each state's electoral votes on the basis of the popular vote in that state instead of the present winner-take-all formula.

The present system is out of keeping with such significant pronouncements as the one-man, one-vote ruling of the U.S. Supreme Court. The simplest approach would be outright abolition of the electoral college system entirely. The direct popular vote then would become the determinant.

An alternative could be the proportional allocation of each state's electoral votes on the basis of the actual popular vote, thus eliminating the existing requirement for all of a state's electoral votes to go to the candidate with the greatest number of popular votes.

The procedure for change is that of a constitutional amendment. In other words, the Congress must enact a resolution by a two-thirds vote of both houses, which must then be ratified by three-fourths of the state legislatures. Constitutional amendments also can be initiated "on application of the Legislatures of two-thirds of the several states" by means of a constitutional convention called by the Congress. But the initiative more likely will come from Washington in this case.

You haven't said much about the governors. What's the outlook for that office?

If a politician has higher ambitions, his election as a state governor is a lot like buying a ticket on the Titanic. Being a governor leads to "a political fatality rate approaching genocide," as writer Richard M. Cohen phrased it in an article in the *Washington Post* in early 1972. The federal government has lowered the tax rate during recent years while states have raised theirs. At a 1972 governors' conference in Houston, Texas, Minnesota Governor Wendell R. Anderson noted the fact and tallied the list of his predecessors who had raised taxes. There wasn't one who was able to advance politically in the aftermath.

The governors are barons of barren fiefdoms because the states have become the orphans of American government and therefore of politics. In the 1960s, the channel was opened directly between the federal government and the cities for the flow of copious funds to the fiscally beleaguered urbanites. That's now happening with the states to a certain degree. A federal–state partnership of sorts is emerging, in other words.

Nevertheless, the office of governor, while still eagerly sought, isn't the best spawning ground for White House hopes—a condition which could be changed, however, by the surfacing of a popular state chief executive.

What about the state legislatures? What does the future hold for them?

A fair statement is that most need to be modernized, and some will be as attention is increasingly focused on their problems and deficiencies.

The landmark analysis, we feel, was produced in 1971 by the Citizens Conference on State Legislatures, titled *The Sometime Governments: A Critical Study of the 50 American Legislatures*. It was published in book form and detailed a comprehensive listing of factors against which the various state legislatures were measured.

The book resulted from a four-year effort which convinced the conference that:

Although improvements were being made, two main barriers stood in the way of rapid progress toward legislative reform. Not enough was known about individual state legislatures—often even by their own members—and information comparing one legislature to another or to all of the others was totally nonexistent. .. . . In addition, the terminology used by legislators, the press, and academics when they attempt to compare legislative procedures is entirely misleading. A "public hearing" on a bill in California bears no resemblance to an activity called by the same name in Massachusetts.

The study identified five characteristics as being required for a legislature to have the "bare necessities of legislative capability." They should be functional, accountable, informed, independent, and representative. Modernization of facilities, adequate staffing, reasonable compensation, adequate time to meet the state's requirements, efficient rules and procedures, and size are key elements of how effective and responsive a legislative body will be.

By the way of illustration, the study concluded that the amount of time allocated to legislatures to function is not well related to their real requirements:

Public problems are essentially open-ended. Issues of health, education, transportation, land use, and law enforcement, to cite a few matters of continuing public concern, never adjourn. They remain public problems whether the legislature is in official session or not, and whether legislators are on salary or not.

A legislature that meets only in biennial session faces formidable problems, most notably in fiscal planning. It is extraordinarily difficult, even under the best of circumstances, to forecast revenues and expenditures six months or a year ahead; it is impossible to do so with any degree of accuracy two or three years ahead. Yet that is what legislatures on a strictly biennial schedule are required to do.

Recognition of this weakness is apparent in changes in the pattern of session schedules, as the study notes: "In 1941, only four state legislatures had regularly scheduled annual sessions; in 1970, there were 31; and those states which are restricted to regularly scheduled biennial sessions—such as Missouri and Washington—have increasingly come to resort to special sessions in the even-numbered years."

Congressman Henry Reuss (D–Wisc.), writing on state and local governments in the year 2000, projects a vastly improved condition of life for the legislatures, including such possibilities as consolidated legislatures of groups of states and an average annual salary for legislators of $35,000, based on the job being full time with annual legislative sessions.

In April 1972, the conference, in its Research Memorandum 15, titled

Legislatures Move to Improve Their Effectiveness, sounded an optimistic note:

> Hundreds of improvements in the state legislative process across the nation since mid-1970—and indications of developments to come —lead to the conclusion that legislatures are strengthening themselves at an accelerating pace.
>
> Actions taken by the legislatures to improve their effectiveness reflect a growing self-awareness and sense of responsibility toward the legislative role. Legislatures are giving themselves more time in which to do their work; they are raising salaries and expense allowances to more realistic levels; they are making their actions more visible and accessible to the public; they are expanding staffs to bolster their capabilities; they are adding space and improving their working surroundings; they are using more computer technology to speed their work. Concurrently, they are reducing the number of committees; limiting the number of committees a legislator may serve on; improving record keeping, bill printing and statutory retrieval systems; and commissioning groups of citizens and/or legislators to make studies and recommend further improvements.
>
> In short, there is a trend toward putting the legislative enterprise on a more realistic and responsible basis.

While that report may sound like the millennium for state legislatures has arrived, it doubtless has not, and it will be more than a few years before the seeds of modernity planted by the conference and other concerned groups will flower and bear fruit. But the momentum obviously has begun and should continue.

And the mayors?

For some of the big-city mayors, that office is almost a sinecure. For others, it's a stopping-off point, occasionally rather brief, before attaining political insignificance if not oblivion. But for very few is it a stepping-stone to major national offices.

Like the governors, the mayors of large cities lead precarious political lives. Defeat comes more easily for these two classes of incumbents than for members of Congress. And when it does, it tends to be more decisive in terms of inability to rebound and run again either for the same office or another, in contrast to the resiliency of congressmen and senators who are brought down.

What about the proposal of the Center for Democratic Institutions for adoption of a new constitution to replace the old one?

The proposal was sponsored by the Center for Democratic Studies and drawn up by Rexford G. Tugwell in consultation with a dozen lawyers, political scientists, sociologists, and others. It is not an amendment to the present Constitution but an entirely new document called the "Constitution of the United Republics of America." It would abolish the fifty states, replacing them with roughly equally populated "republics." It would retain the office of presidency and add a second vice-president, limiting the terms of each to six years instead of the present two four-year terms.

The plan would also prohibit private financing of election campaigns. Instead, each taxpayer would be surcharged an extra 1 percent of his income taxes to help pay for the campaigns.

Is all of this a good idea?

Some of it is and most isn't, in our opinion. We can't see valid reasons at this time for a new Constitution, nor for abolition of the fifty states, nor for adding a second vice-president and limiting the presidential office to one six-year term. We feel that accountability of a president and his party to the people every four years is reasonable. Six years would be too long a span for an unpopular president with unpopular policies. At the same time, a popular president would have available to him a possible second term to continue what he has started.

The idea of federal financing of election campaigns ties in with the plan already on the books enabling the taxpayer after 1973 and beyond to indicate on his tax form whether he wants $1.00 of his money to go into the campaign coffers of one or the other political parties. We like this approach better than adding a 1 percent surcharge onto the taxpayer's already high tab.

What ideas do you have for getting better candidates to run for public office in the future?

Better than our view, we cite the findings of Dr. George Gallup whose surveys reveal that an extraordinary number of citizens from all fields of endeavor would be willing to run for public office, from the mayor of their hometown to the presidency, upon certain conditions. Specifically, they would become candidates:

1. If they were asked to run by a committee of responsible citizens after due investigation.

2. If they did not have to raise their own campaign funds.

3. If they did not have to serve for more than a limited period of time and could return to their profession or calling after their time in office.

4. If they did not have to take orders from a political boss but could represent what they considered the nation's best interests.

These conditions, Dr. Gallup says, would help to bring into public office men and women of the highest talent. He adds, "A fair estimate, based upon poll findings, is that at least half of our ablest citizens would serve in public office under these conditions."

Okay, what's being done to meet the conditions Gallup outlines?

Depends. For instance:

On point no. 1, since candidates are selected in most areas by party primaries, the support of committees of responsible citizens could be helpful, but not decisive, in their election. In other words, the citizens committee doesn't have it in its power to appoint a candidate on its own and assure his nomination or election. He still has to meet the test of his party's voters in a primary contest and the public in the general election.

On point no. 2, if the $1.00 income tax checkoff plan is extended to all federal elections, it would take a big burden off the backs of candidates for the U.S. Senate and House. Candidates for state and local offices would still have to raise their own funds locally, however.

On point no. 3, despite a candidate's initial decision to stay in office only for a limited time, he might like it after a while and become reluctant to bow out. However, since there is no law which says a candidate has to serve more terms than he wants, he is literally free to return to his profession or calling when he wants to and to let someone else run in his place.

Point no. 4 is less valid today than it might once have been. In fact, any candidate elected on the basis of the three preceding points shouldn't have to be concerned about the last one.

Selected bibliography

Alexander, Dr. Herbert E. *Financing the 1968 Election*. Lexington, Mass.: Heath-Lexington Books, 1971.

American Academy of Arts and Sciences. *The Future of the United States Government: Toward the Year 2000*. Edited by Harvey S. Perloff. New York: George Braziller, 1971.

The American Assembly. *The Congress and America's Future*. Edited by David B. Truman. Englewood Cliffs, N.J.: Prentice-Hall, 1965.

Bolling, Richard. *Power in the House*. New York: Macmillan, 1964.

Bonitati, Robert F., ed. *Winning Campaigns*. New York: Popular Library, 1971.

Broder, David S. *The Party's Over: The Failure of Politics in America*. New York: Harper & Row, 1971, 1972.

Burkhalter, Everett, as quoted in the *Washington Post*, April 3, 1964.

Celler, Emanuel. "The Seniority Rule in Congress," *Western Political Quarterly*, March 1961, pp. 160–167.

Citizens Conference on State Legislatures. *The Sometime Governments: A Critical Study of the 50 American Legislatures*. Written by John Burns. New York: Bantam, 1971.

Clapp, Charles L. *The Congressman: His Work as He Sees It*. Garden City, New York: Doubleday, 1964.

Cleveland, James C. *We Propose: A Modern Congress*. Ed. by Mary McInnis. New York: McGraw-Hill, 1966.

David, Dr. Paul T. *Party Strength in the United States, 1872–1970*. Charlottesville, Va.: University Press of Virginia, 1972.

215

Democratic Study Group. "The Seniority System in the U.S. House of Representatives." *Special Report*, February 25, 1970.

Dunn, Delmer D. "Highlights of Financing Presidential Campaigns." *Brookings Research Report 125*, 1972.

Evry, Hal. *The Selling of a Candidate*. Los Angeles: Western Opinion Research Center, 1971.

Galloway, George B. *Congress at the Crossroads*. New York: T. Y. Crowell, 1946.

Galloway, George B. *History of the House of Representatives*. New York: T. Y. Crowell, 1962.

Galloway, George B. *The Legislative Process in Congress*. New York: T. Y. Crowell, 1953.

Gallup, George. *The Sophisticated Poll Watcher's Guide*. Princeton, N.J.: Princeton Opinion Press, 1972.

Gardner, John. *No Easy Victories*. New York: Harper & Row, 1968.

Goodwin, George, Jr. "The Seniority System in Congress." *American Political Science Review*, June 1959, pp. 412–436.

Gough, G. W. *Economic Consequences of Socialism*. London: P. Allan & Co., Ltd., 1926.

Greenstein, Fred I. *The American Party System and the American People*. Englewood Cliffs, N.J.: Prentice-Hall, 1970.

Griffith, Ernest S. *Congress: Its Contemporary Role*. 3rd ed. New York: New York University Press, 1961.

Hess, Robert D., and Judith V. Torney. *The Development of Political Attitudes in Children*. Chicago: Aldine, 1967.

Hess, Stephen, and Milton Kaplan. *The Ungentlemanly Art*. New York: Macmillan, 1968.

Hiebert, Ray, et al., eds. *The Political Image Merchants: Strategies in the New Politics*. Washington, D.C.: Acropolis Books, 1971.

Jennings, M. Kent, and Richard G. Niemi. "The Transmission of Political Values from Parent to Child." *American Political Science Review*, Vol. 62, March 1968.

Lahr, Raymond M., and J. William Theis. *Congress: Power and Purpose on Capitol Hill*. Boston: Allyn & Bacon, 1967.

League of Women Voters of the United States. *Choosing the President*. Washington, D.C.: League of Women Voters, 1968.

Levy, Mark R., and Michael S. Kramer. *The Ethnic Factor: How America's Minorities Decide Elections*. New York: Simon & Schuster, 1972 (for the Institute of American Research, Inc.).

Lubbell, Samuel. *The Hidden Crisis in American Politics*. New York: W. W. Norton, 1970.

McNeil, Neil. *Forge of Democracy: The House of Representatives*. New York: David McKay, 1964.

Miller, Clem. *Member of the House: Letters of a Congressman*. New York: Scribner's, 1962.

Neustadt, Richard E. *Presidential Power: The Politics of Leadership*. New York and Toronto: New American Library, 1964.

Nimmo, Dan. *The Political Persuaders*. Englewood Cliffs, N.J.: Prentice-Hall, 1970.

Parkinson, Hank. *Winning Your Campaign*. Englewood Cliffs, N.J.: Prentice-Hall, 1970.

Parris, Judith H. *The Convention Problem*. Report 127. Washington, D.C.: Brookings Institution, 1972.

Penniman, Howard R. "Financing Campaigns in the Public Interest." In *Campaign Finances*, a special analysis for The American Enterprise Institute for Public Policy Research, 1971.

Pohl, Frederick. *Practical Politics 1972*. New York: Ballantine Books, 1971.

Polsby, Nelson W., and Aaron B. Wildavsky. *Presidential Elections: Strategies of American Electoral Politics*. 2nd ed. New York: Scribner's, 1968.

Pomper, Gerald M. *Elections in America*. New York: Dodd, Mead, 1968.

Riegle, Donald. *O Congress*. New York: Doubleday, 1972.

Ripley, Randall B. *Power in the Senate*. New York: St. Martin's Press, 1969.

Safire, William. *The New Language of Politics*. New York: Random House, 1968.

Scammon, Richard M., and Ben J. Wattenberg. *The Real Majority*. New York: Coward-McCann, 1970.

Scott, Hugh D. *How to Go into Politics*. New York: John Day, 1949.

Shadegg, Stephen C. *How to Win an Election: The Art of Political Victory*. New York: Taplinger, 1964.

Stimpson, George. *A Book About American Politics*. New York: Harper & Brothers, 1952.

Tacheron, Donald G., and Morris K. Udall. *The Job of the Congressman*. 2nd ed. Indianapolis and New York: Bobbs-Merrill, 1970.

Theis, Paul A., and Edmund L. Henshaw. *Who's Who in American Politics*. 3rd ed. New York: R. R. Bowker, 1971.

U.S. News & World Report. *U.S. Politics—Inside and Out*. Toronto: Collier-Macmillan, 1970.

White, Theodore H. *The Making of the President, 1968*. New York: Atheneum, 1969.

Index

Adams, John, 14, 26, 27, 183
Adams, John Quincy, 18, 28, 101, 173, 177
Advise and consent, 144
Agnew, Spiro T., 10, 111
Aiken, Sen. George, 138, 195, 203
Alexander, Dr. Herbert E., 103–105
American Conservative Union, 46
American Enterprise Institute for Public Policy Research, 104, 152
American Independent Party, 26
American Legion, 17, 128
American Medical Association, 17
American party, 26
American Party System and the American People, 85
American Political Science Review, 85
Americans for Constitutional Action, 40
Americans for Democratic Action, 40, 46
Anderson, Wendell R., 210
Anti-Federalist Republicans, 26, 27
Anti-Mason party, 33

Baker v. Carr, 86
Bandwagon theory, 102

Banks, Nathaniel P., 151
Beveridge, Albert J., 92
Bierce, Ambrose, 18
Bills
    administration bills, 142
    become an act, 141
    discharge petitions, 143
    pigeon-holed, 141
    public law, 141
    rider, 143, 144
Bismarck, Chancellor of Prussia, 9
Black Congressional Caucus, 194
Blacks
    chairman of a national political convention, 170
    elected officials, 82
    political power, 193, 194
    vote, 81, 82
Bloc voting
    blacks, 77, 81, 82
    Catholics, 77, 84
    elderly, 84
    farmers, 81
    poor, 77
    Protestant, 77, 84
    women, 82, 83
    youth, 77
Bolling, Rep. Richard, 147

Bond, Julian, 194
Border states, 79
Bossism, 14, 15
Boston Centinel, 77, 78
Bovay, A. E., 29
Brademas, Rep. John, 186, 187, 200
Broder, David S., 4, 63, 189
Brookings Institution, 208
Brown, B. Gratz, 18
Bruce, Blanche Kelso, 170
Bryan, William Jennings, 95
Buchanan, James, 184
Buckley, Sen. James, 48, 63, 151, 152
Bull Moose Convention of 1912, 47, 92
Burke, Edmund, 136
Burkhalter, Rep. Everett G., 149
Burleson, Albert, 8
Burr, Aaron, 15
Byrd, Sen. Harry F., 151, 152

Campaign Reform Bill. *See* Federal
    Election Campaign Act of 1971
Campaigning, 65, 66, 89, 91, 92
    advantages of being an incumbent,
        103
    advertising, 90, 96
    announcing candidacy, 92, 93
    campaign workers, 90
    direct mail, 90
    future, 194–199
    ghost writers, 110, 111
    grand strategy, 90
    guidelines, 20, 65, 93, 94, 101, 109
    humor, 111
    image, 95
    issues, 98
    master plan, 90
    media, 90, 97, 98, 105
    packaging a candidate, 95
    party leaders, 66
    peaking, 90, 91
    personal contacts, 90
    public relations, 96
    publicity activities, 90, 96
    selling the candidate, 94
    smear, 108, 109, 111

Campaigning (Cont.)
    spending levels, 103–105, 107, 113
    wife's role, 94
    winning, 86
Cannon, Joseph G., 66
Canvass, 91, 92
Caraway, Mrs. Hattie, 158
Carpetbagger, 15, 16, 79
Caucus, 15
Celler, Rep. Emanuel, 138, 147
Center, political, 20
Center for Democratic Institutions,
    213
Check swap, 197
Check-off funds. *See* Revenue Act of
    1971
Checks and balances, 159
Citizens Conference of State Legisla-
    tion, 210
Citizens Research Foundation, 104
Civil service system, 8, 15
Clapp, Charles L., 143
Clark, John C., 18
Clay, Sen. Henry, 185
Cleveland, Grover, 7, 174, 184
Coattail theory, 181
Cohen, Richard, 210
Communications Act of 1934, 115
Communism, 22
Congress
    club rule, 157
    Committee on the Committees, 146
    courtesy, 157
    districts, 153, 154
    immunity, 157
    joint committee, 142
    rider, 143, 144
    Standards of Official Conduct Com-
        mittee, 128
    standing committee, 142
    subcommittee, 142
Congress at the Crossroads, 148
Congressional Record, 140, 157
Congressman, The, 143
Conservative
    definition, 17–20
    percent of population, 20
Conservative Establishment, 17
Conservative party, 26

Constitution of the United Republics of America, 213
Constitution of the United States
checks and balances, 159
electoral reform amendment, 209
national primary amendment, 203
nineteenth amendment, 179, 180
seventeenth amendment, 44, 154
twentieth amendment, 151, 171
twenty-third amendment, 172
Constitutional Union party, 26
Convention Problem, 208
Coolidge, Calvin, 92, 200
Costykian, Edward, 8
Crawford, Kenneth, 206

Daley, Richard, 15, 208
Dark horse, 176
David, Paul T., 79
Davis, John W., 170
Dawson, Paul, 107
Dayton, William L., 31, 32
Demagogue, 23
Democracy, 21, 22
Democratic party
Congress, 48, 49
Congressional Committee, 45
discipline, 42
Governors Caucus, 45, 46
history, 26–29
national chairmen, 43
National Committee, 41–43
party policy, 40
party symbols, 33, 35, 36
philosophy, 38, 39, 40
platform, 38
Senatorial Campaign Committee, 45
state and local organizations, 41, 42, 49
state chairmen, 43
statistics on, 47, 48
See also Johnson, Lyndon B.; Kennedy, John F.; Political parties; Roosevelt, Franklin D.
Development of Political Attitudes in Children, 85
Dewey, John, 13

Dewey, Thomas E., 102
Dole, Sen. Robert, vii–viii, 43, 123
Dollar-a-year man, 64
Dominick, Sen. Peter H., 45
Douglass, Frederick, 177, 178
Dove, 24

Eagleton, Sen. Thomas F., 171
Eastern Establishment, 17
Economic Consequences of Socialism, 22
Eisenhower, Dwight D., 109
election of 1952, 48, 79, 80
election of 1956, 47, 48, 79, 80, 181, 194
view of the presidency, 185
Election bets, 130, 131
Election day, 87, 88
Election Reform Law, 118
Elections
general, 61–63
primary, 61
Elections in America, 37
Electoral College, 171–174, 209
Ellender, Sen. Allen, 138
Equal time, 125–128
Ethnic Factor: How American Minorities Decide Elections, 193
Ethnic voters. *See* Voting blocs
Evry, Hal, 73

Fair Campaign Practices Committee, 109
Fairness doctrine, 127, 128
Farm Bureau, 17
Farm vote, 81
Fatal 20s theory, 174, 175
Favorite son, 162
Favoritism, 8
Federal Communications Act of 1934, 125
Federal Communications Commission, 125, 127
Federal Corrupt Practices Act of 1925, 119, 120
Federal Election Campaign Act of 1971, 106, 113

Federal Election Campaign Act of
1971 (Cont.)
advertising, 115, 116
contributions, 113, 117, 118, 120
media, 114, 115
spending limitations, 113–116
Federalist, The, 159
Federalists, 26, 27
Fellow travelers, 23
Felton, Rebecca, 158
Field Piece, 33
Filibuster, 144
*Financing Campaigns in the Public
Interest*, 152
*Financing Parties and Campaigns in
1968*, 103, 105
Ford, Rep. Gerald R., 203
Franklin, Benjamin, 22
Fremont, John C., 31, 32
French National Assembly, 20
Future changes in political practice
better candidates, 213, 214
black political power, 193, 194
campaigns, 194–199
Congress, 200–202
Constitution, 213
conventions, 209
Electoral College, 209
electorate, 192
ethnic voters, 193
governors, 210
mayors, 212
party realignment, 190, 191
political parties, 188–190
political system, 186, 187
presidential primary, 203–208
president's role, 199, 200
seniority system, 201, 202
state legislatures, 210–212
third and fourth parties, 191, 192
vice-presidential candidates, 205,
206
*Future of the U.S. Government:
Toward the Year 2000*, 186

Galloway, George, 148, 151, 160
Gallup, Dr. George, 213, 214
Gallup Poll
accuracy, 101

Gallup Poll (Cont.)
better candidates, 213, 214
campaign reform, 113
independent voters, 47
most admired Americans (1971), 10
party breakdown (1972), 47
political philosophy of adults (1972),
76
political philosophy of youth (1972),
75, 76
reliability, 101
samplings, 100
single presidential primary (1972),
205
Gardner, John, 188
Garfield, James A., 174, 176, 184
General elections, 61, 63
George, David Lloyd, 10
Gerry, Elbridge, 77, 78
Gerrymander, 77, 78
Goldberg, Rube, 80, 110, 207
Goldwater, Sen. Barry, 17, 47, 79, 111,
181, 199
Gough, G. W., 22
Governorships, 48
Graham, Rev. Billy, 10
Grant, Ulysses S., 18
Grassroots, 92
Greeley, Horace, 18, 19, 29
Greenstein, Fred I., 85
Greider, William, 16
Gross National Product, 104

Hall, Leonard, 109
Hallett, B. P., 41
Hamilton, Alexander, 27, 172
Hanna, Mark, 95
Harding, Warren G., 66, 79, 174
Harper's Weekly, 33–35
Harris, Louis, 20, 192
Harris Poll
attitudes toward politicians (1972),
10
political center (1972), 20
reliability, 101
samplings, 100
Harrison, Benjamin, 7, 174
Harrison, William Henry, 102, 174,
176

Hartford Courant, 21
Hat in the ring, 67, 68
Hatch Act, 116, 117
Hawk, 24
Hayes, Rutherford B., 62, 174
Hess, Robert D., 85
Hill, George Washington, 105
History of the House of Representatives, 151, 160
Hollings, Sen. Ernest, 45
Hope, Bob, 10
House Democratic Study Group, 147–149
House of Representatives
  allowances, 155, 156
  attendance, 145
  average age, 138
  background, 138
  bills, 141–144
  business influence, 145, 146
  Congressional Districts, 153, 154
  courtesy and immunity, 157
  impeachment, 158
  labor influence, 145, 146
  lame-duck Congress, 150–151
  lobbyists, 145
  mail, 138–140
  national interest vs. constituencies, 135
  organizational vote, 153
  replacements, 154, 155
  requirements for membership, 136
  retirement, 156
  salaries, 53
  seniority system, 146–150
  sessions, 140
  terms, 137, 202
  title, 137
  turnover, 152, 153
  two-party system, 151, 152
  women members, 158
Howell, Henry R., 105, 107
Humphrey, Sen. Hubert H., 10
  election of 1968, 46, 84, 102–104

Image, 95
Independent voters, 47, 48, 61, 63, 64
Ingalls, John J., 91
Involvement. *See* Political involvement

Jackson, Andrew, 7, 28, 101, 177
Jefferson, Thomas, 24, 27, 173, 184
Jennings, M. Kent, 85
Job of the Congressman, 129, 131
Johnson, Linea W., 177
Johnson, Lyndon B., 10
  election of 1960, 21, 111
  election of 1964, 181
  election of 1968, 52, 105
  populist, 16
  view of the presidency, 185
Johnson, Richard, 173
Journal of the American Medical Association, 111

Kansas–Nebraska Bill, 29
Kennedy, Sen. Edward M., 10
Kennedy, John F.
  background, 174, 176, 177
  Catholic, 91, 177
  election of 1960, 21, 62, 82, 111, 128
Kennedy, Robert F., 105
Kerch, Charles G., 99
Kingmakers, 16
Knott, John, 83
Kramer, Michael S., 193

Labor unions, 145, 146
La Follette, Robert M., 46
La Guardia, Fiorello, 151
Lame duck, 150, 151, 173
Landon, Alf, 47
Left, the, 20, 21
Legislative Process in Congress, 148
Legislatures Move to Improve Their Effectiveness, 212
Lerner, Max, 23
Levy, Mark R., 193
Liberal
  definition, 17–20
  percent of population, 20
Liberal party, 26
Liberal Republican Party, 18, 19
Limiting Congressional terms, 203
Lincoln, Abraham, 13, 31–33, 79, 95, 174, 176, 184

Lindsay, John V., 17, 51, 148
Lippmann, Walter, 4
Lobbyists, 145
Local party
  building up, 59, 60
  structure, 59, 60
Lockwood, Belva Ann Bennett, 177
Lodge, Henry Cabot, 21
Lowenstein, Allard, 52
Lunatic fringe, 21
Lynch, John Roy, 170

McCarthy, Sen. Eugene, 105
McCarthy, Sen. Joseph R., 22, 23
McCarthyism, 22, 23
McDonald, Dr. Lee C., 7
McGovern, Sen. George, 39, 105, 169
Machine politics, 13
McKinley, William, 95, 174, 176, 177
Madison, James, 24, 159
Maguson, Sen. Warren, 16
Majority, 73
Making of the President, 91
Mandel, Gov. Marvin, 46
Manning, Reg, 108
Mansfield, Sen. Mike, 195, 203
Mansfield-Aiken Plan, 195, 204, 206
Marcy, Sen. William, 7
Marginal districts, 154
Mason, James, 18
Mathis, Dawson, 138
Media, 90, 97, 98, 105
Meet the Press, 192
Middle-of-the-roaders, 20
Milliken, Gov. William G., 45
Minority voters. See Bloc voting; Voting
Morgan, Edwin D., 41
Moynihan, Patrick Daniel, 187
My Summer in a Garden, 21

Nader, Ralph, 10, 119
Nast, Thomas, 33–36
Nation, The, 21
National committees, 41–46

National conventions
  convention site, 166
  delegates, 166–169
  future, 203–209
  necessity of, 167
  origin, 165
  two-thirds rule, 169
  unit rule, 169
National party, 26
Native son, 162
Negroes. See Blacks
Neustadt, Richard E., 161
Newberry v. U.S., 120
New Harper's Monthly, 25
New Language of Politics, The, 14, 111
New Politics, 11, 13
New Republic, 197
New York Tribune, 29, 32
New York World, 91
Niemi, Richard G., 85
Nineteenth Constitutional Amendment, 179, 180
Nixon, Richard M., 8, 109, 123, 204
  election of 1960, 17, 62, 79, 82, 128
  election of 1968, 46, 71, 79, 82, 102–105
  Federal Elections Campaign Act., 119
  ideal politician, definition of, 6
  most admired American, 10
  Ninety-first Congress, 181
  philosophical stand, 39
  silent majority, 24
  Supreme Court appointments, 144
No Easy Victory, 188
Norris, George W., 151

O'Brien, Lawrence, 90
O Congress, 135
O'Conor, Charles, 177
Off-year voting, 72
One man, one vote, 85, 86
O'Neill, Rep. Thomas P., 45
Orben, Robert, 111
Organization, political, 13
Organizational vote, 153

Packaging a candidate, 95
Packwood, Sen. Robert, 195, 206
Page, Walter Hines, 25
Parkinson, Hank, 90
Parris, Judith, 208
Party Strength in the United States, 1872–1970, 79
Party's Over, The, 4, 63, 189
Pastore, Sen. John O., 123
Peace and Freedom party, 26
Penniman, Howard R., 104, 152
Platforms, 33, 35, 37, 38
Plurality, 73
Pohl, Frederick, 52, 64
Pol, 5
Political Activities Act of 1939, 116
Political bosses, 14
Political involvement, 51–55
Political parties, 26
   differences, 38–40
   financing, 44
   national committees, 41–46
   necessity of, 49, 50
   party realignments, 190, 191
   philosophies, 38–40, 76
   platform, 33, 35, 37, 38
   policy, 40
   state and local level, 41, 42
   strength, 47
   symbols, 33–36
   third and fourth parties, 46
   two-party system, 26, 27
Politicians
   complaints against, 10
   definition, 5, 6, 9–11
   qualities of, 5
   salaries, 52, 53
   statistics, 9
Politics, 3, 6
   definition, 5, 9
   favoritism, 8
   machine, 13
   motivation into, 4
   New, 11, 13
   power, 11
Polk, James Knox, 176, 184
Polls
   bandwagon theory, 102
   cost, 99

Polls (Cont.)
   Gallup. *See* Gallup Poll
   Harris. *See* Harris Poll
   issues, 98
   origin, 101, 102
   supermarket poll, 99, 100
Polls, election, 109
Pomper, Gerald M., 37, 38
Populism, 16
Populist party, 16
Power of the House, 147
Power in the Senate, 147
Power politics, 11
Practical politics, 1972, 52, 64
President
   Catholic, 177
   checks and balances, 159
   coattail theory, 181
   Congress, 170, 179, 181, 182
   dark horse, 176
   Electoral College, 171–174
   facts about past presidents, 162–164, 170
   fatal 20s theory, 174, 175
   favorite son, 162
   incumbents' chances, 163
   native sons, 162
   power of, 160, 161
   presidents view their job, 182–185
   primaries, 166–169, 203–209
   replacement, 171, 174
   requirements, 161
   salary, 52, 53, 182
   Twentieth Amendment, 151, 171
   unit rule of selection, 169
   vice-presidents become presidents, 164
   women candidates, 177
Presidential Election Campaign Fund, 124, 125
Presidential Power, 161
Presidential primaries, 166–169, 203–209
Primary elections, 61
Procter and Gamble, 104
Progressive party, 46, 47
Prohibition party, 26
Public Citizens, Inc., 119
Public Opinion Quarterly, 107

Public relations and publicity, 96
Purves, Dr. Pierre, 71

Radical Republicans, 18
Rankin, Jeanette, 158
Reagan, Gov. Ronald, 105
Real Majority, The, 20, 39, 47, 95
Reed, Rep. Thomas Brackett, 11, 12
Registration, 86
Reiter, Howard L., 190
Republic, 21, 22
Republican party
  Congress, 48, 49
  Congressional Committee, 44
  discipline, 42
  Governors Association, 45
  Grand Old Party (GOP), 32, 33
  history, 26, 27, 29–32
  national chairmen, 43
  national committee, 41–43
  party policy, 40
  philosophy, 38–40
  platform, 38
  Senatorial Campaign Committee,
    44–45
  state and local organizations, 41, 42,
    49
  state chairmen, 41, 43
  statistics, 47, 48
  symbol, 33, 36
  See also Eisenhower, Dwight D.;
    Nixon, Richard M.; Political
    parties
Research Report, 127, 208
Reuss, Rep. Henry, 211
Revenue Act of 1971, 120–125
Reynolds v. Sims, 86
Riegle, Rep. Donald, 135
Right, The, 20, 21
Ripley, Randall B., 147
Ripon College, 29
Ripon Forum, 190
Ripon Society, 46
Robertson, Alice M., 158
Roche, John P., 91
Rockefeller, Gov. Nelson, 17, 63, 105
Rockefeller, Gov. Winthrop, 194
Rogers, Will, 102

Romney, Gov. George, 105, 161
Roosevelt, Franklin D., 174, 176
  election of 1932, 25, 67, 170
  election of 1936, 47
  party realignment, 190
  view of the presidency, 185
Roosevelt, Theodore
  background, 123, 177
  election of 1912, 67, 68
  lunatic fringe, 21
  view of the presidency, 184
Rumsfeld, Donald, 156

Safire, William, 14, 111
Scammon, Richard M., 20, 39, 47,
  48, 95
Scott, Sen. Hugh, 135
Selden, John, 112
Selling of a Candidate, The, 73
Senate
  advise and consent, 144
  allowances, 155, 156
  attendance, 138
  background, 138
  bills, 141–144
  business influence, 145, 146
  courtesy and immunity, 157
  filibuster, 144
  impeachment, 158
  labor influence, 145, 146
  lame-duck Congress, 150, 151
  lobbyists, 145
  mail, 138–140
  national interests vs. constituencies,
    135
  replacement, 154, 155
  requirements of membership, 136
  retirement, 155
  salary, 53
  seniority system, 146–150
  sessions, 140
  Seventeenth Constitutional Amend-
    ment, 44, 154
  term, 137, 202
  title, 137
  two-party system, 151, 152
  women members, 158
Seniority Rule in Congress, 147

Seniority system, 146–150
Seniority System in Congress, 148
Seventeenth Constitutional Amendment, 44, 154
Shakespeare, William, 21, 66
Sherman, Gen. William T., 176, 177
Sherman, James S., 171
Sherman-like statement, 176, 177
Silent majority, 24
Smear, 108, 109, 111
Smith, Alfred E., 170, 177
Smith, Sen. Margaret Chase, 52, 177
Smith, Rep. T. V., 52
Socialism, 22
Socialist Labor party, 26
Socialist Workers party, 26
Solid South, 79
Sometimes Government, The: A Critical Study of 50 American Legislatures, 210
Spoils system, 7
Stalking horse, 176
Stanton, Frank, 126, 127
Stassen, Harold, 105
State legislatures, 49, 210–212
Statesman, 11
Stevenson, Adlai E., 47, 181
Student's Guide to Practical Politics, 7
Stylistic populism, 16
Sumner, William Graham, 24
Sundquist, James L., 186
Supermarket poll, 99, 100
Survey Research Center of the University of Michigan, 46
Swing district, 154

Tacheron, Donald G., 129
Taft, William Howard, 171
Tammany Hall, 8, 14, 15, 98
Target district, 154
Tax check-off. *See* Revenue Act of 1971
Taylor, Zachary, 174
Television debates, 128
Tempest, The, 21
Third and fourth parties, 46, 151, 152, 191, 192
Thurmond, Sen. Strom, 47

Ticket-splitting, 62, 63
Tilden, Samuel, 174
Torney, Judith V., 85
Tory, 17, 18
Transmission of Political Values from Parent to Child, 85
Truman, Harry S, 185, 204
background, 109
election of 1948, 101
statesman, 11
Tugwell, Rexford G., 213
Tunney, Sen. John, 138
Tweed, William Marcy, 14, 15
Twentieth Century Fund Commission on Costs in the Electronic Era, 105
Twentieth Constitutional Amendment, 151, 171
Twenty-third Constitutional Amendment, 172
Two-party system, 26, 27, 151, 152
Two-thirds rule, 169

Udall, Rep. Morris, 129
Unit rule, 169
U.S. Census Bureau, 73, 84, 100, 114
U.S. v. Classic, 120

Van Buren, Martin, 7, 18, 33, 36, 173, 176
Vice-presidency, 164, 174, 179
Volunteers, political, 53–55, 57–59
experience, 56, 57
recruitment, 56, 60
Voting, 62
average voter, 73, 74
blocs, 77, 81
decision, 74
definition, 87
eighteen-year-olds, 75, 76
eligibility, 74, 86
new voters, 75, 76
off years, 72
participation, 71, 72
party preference, 75, 84, 85
population, 76, 77
registration, 86

Voting (Cont.)
  requirements, 73
  residency, 81, 86
  rights for criminals, 86, 87
  turnout, 71, 72
  twenty-one year limit, 75, 76

Wallace, Gov. George C., 10
  election of 1968, 26, 46, 104
  populism, 16
  tax check-off benefit, 122
  third and fourth parties, 191
Wallace, Henry A., 47
Warner, Charles Dudley, 21
Washington, George, 26, 182
Washington Post, 4, 16, 149, 206, 210
Watchdog theory, 63
Wattenberg, Ben J., 20, 39, 47, 48,
  95

We Propose: A Modern Congress, 148
Wesberry v. Sanders, 86
Westwood, Mrs. Jean, ix–x, 43
White, Theodore, 91
Who's Who in American Politics, 9
Wilson, Rep. Bob, 44
Wilson, Woodrow, 8, 184
Winning Your Campaign, 90
Women
  in Congress, 158
  presidential candidates, 177
  suffrage, 179
  voters, 82, 83
Woodhull, Mrs. Victoria Claflin, 177,
  178

Youth vote, 74–76

Zinser, James, 107